PUBLICATIONS OF THE
SCOTTISH COUNCIL FOR RESEARCH IN EDUCATION
62

A STUDY OF FIFTEEN-YEAR-OLDS

A STUDY OF
FIFTEEN-YEAR-OLDS

UNIVERSITY OF LONDON PRESS LTD

ISBN 0 340 11649 8

University of London Press Ltd
St Paul's House, Warwick Lane, London EC4

Printed and bound in Great Britain by
T and A Constable Ltd, Hopetoun Street, Edinburgh EH7 4NF

CONTENTS

PREFACE

The Scottish fifteen-year-olds described in this research formed an age group drawn from a city, some rural areas and the industrial part of a large county. At the beginning of this study some were in junior secondary and the others in senior secondary courses. About the time they reached the age of fifteen all of them were given tests of attainment in language and arithmetic. After the lapse of ten months, endeavour was made to get in touch with them so that they might attempt the same tests for a second time. Some left school to start work in this interval, others continued in full time education. In the event half of the original number were persuaded to attempt the test papers again.

Their scores in these tests are given in this report and these are related to the type of secondary course followed, to their employment preferences at fifteen years of age, to the actual jobs or courses of education they were in when they neared sixteen, to their leisure time interests, to some of their attitudes and to socio-economic factors.

The material recorded in this book provides a description of young people between fifteen and sixteen years of age towards the end of the period in which secondary education was provided mainly in separate junior and senior secondary schools.

GEORGE REITH
Convener

COMMITTEE

G Reith, MA, BSc, MEd, PhD, FEIS, Director of Education for Edinburgh, *Convener*

D McMahon, MA, Applied Psychology Unit, University of Edinburgh

J Meiklejohn, MA, BSc, MEd, PhD, LRAM, ATCL, Director of Education for East Lothian

J G Morris, MA, MEd, HMI, Scottish Education Department

J Sutherland, MA, MEd, PhD, *formerly* Department of Education, Moray House College of Education

ARITHMETIC PANEL

J Sutherland, MA, MEd, PhD, *Convener*

J Baird, MA, BSc, *formerly* Moray House College of Education

*S L Christie, BSc, ARIC, Headmaster, Burntisland Secondary School

W M Herbison, JP, BSc, FEIS, Headmaster, Larkhall Academy

H G Mooney, MA, *formerly* North Berwick High School

J W Trevor Smith, *formerly* Morton Academy, Thornhill

* Died 10 May 1969

ENGLISH PANEL

J G Morris, MA, MEd, HMI, *Convener*

D E Campbell, MA, *formerly* David Kilpatrick Secondary School, Edinburgh

M Carty, MA, St Bride's RC Junior Secondary School, Cambuslang

N Chalmers, MA, *formerly* Portobello Secondary School

R M Greaves, MA, Headmaster, Tranent Public School

W F McCorkindale, MA, *formerly* Annan Academy

J R Rollo, MA, *formerly* Headmaster, Viewforth School, Kirkcaldy

D A Walker, OBE, MA, MEd, PhD, FRSE, FEIS, Director of
the Council
G J Pollock, MA, MEd, AInstP, Depute Director of the Council
Mrs Mary Gray, MA, MEd, Research Officer
Miss Jessie M Gray, MA, Secretary

ANALYSIS OF CONTENTS

LIST OF TABLES

(In these tables percentages are recorded to the nearest whole number and so do not always add up to 100.)

2

LIST OF FIGURES

Chapter 1

ORIGIN OF THE INVESTIGATION

The investigation reported in this volume began as a limited inquiry into the retention of facts and skills learned at school. It arose from the comments of some employers regarding the educational standards of young people entering industry. According to the opinions of some, the schools were not producing enough young people with the standard of education that industry required, pupils of ordinary ability had apparently not been educated to the fullest extent of their abilities and aptitudes, young people were not reaching a level of attainment at school which would enable them to undertake the appropriate training in industry.

One suggestion that had been made in reply to these comments was that the young people were taught the skills at school but in the transfer from school to work had allowed their skills to deteriorate. This suggestion probably arose from the findings of Dr J Sutherland who showed that pupils transferring from primary to secondary education lost a substantial amount of their skills in arithmetic during the early years of the secondary course. This he attributed partly to lack of practice in their skills and partly to lack of incentive to make high scores in tests used in the secondary school.[1]

It was decided that an investigation should be made of the gains and losses in the basic skills in the period immediately following departure from school. In accordance with its usual practice the Council set up a committee to plan and conduct an inquiry into the problem.

After several pilot investigations had been completed, the Committee decided that the appropriate course of action would

[1] 'A comparison of pupils' arithmetical ability in the secondary school with their ability at the time of their transfer from primary schools', J Sutherland, *British Journal of Educational Psychology*, XXI, Pt 1, February 1951, pp 3–8.

be to apply in the summer term of 1960 a set of tests in the basic skills of English and arithmetic to a group of pupils nearing the age when they would be free to leave school and to re-test as many as possible of them a year later in 1961. When this intention was reported to the Executive of the Council that body asked the Committee to take the opportunity to collect as much information as possible about the young people and their transfer from school to work with a view to throwing light on changes that might be found in their attainments during the year.

This they did by asking the young people to complete in 1960 a sociological schedule giving information about home background, job preference, and reason for leaving school, if that was the intention. In 1961, each of those who attended for the re-testing session completed a further questionnaire, giving information about education, occupation, leisure interests and activities, and job preference at a later age.

The field work was completed in 1961 and the first part of the analysis by 1963. The results of this analysis caused a major change in the trend of the investigation and gave rise to the need for a further set of analyses. At that time, proposals were afoot nationally for major changes in secondary school organisation, along with the prospect of the raising of the minimum school-leaving age. Large changes had also been taking place in the approaches to the acquisition of skills in the primary school and changes in method and content at the secondary stage were being recommended. Because of these factors the Committee was hesitant about submitting the report to the Council with a view to publication, there being the possibility of its contents being irrelevant to the new circumstances.

The further set of analyses was nonetheless proceeded with and the Council decided that the report was worthy of publication, giving as it does a picture of young people immediately before and soon after the age at which they were free to leave school, in an era when secondary pupils were allocated to senior secondary and junior secondary courses, and when the introduction of the decimal system into the country's coinage and into industry had not begun. Apart from the intrinsic interest it has as a study of young people, it will, it is hoped, provide a base-line for at least some kinds of comparison in later years when the new systems have been in operation for a sufficiently long period to provide their own data.

The various chapters of this book describe the methods of selecting the sample to be tested, the method of construction of the tests, and the results obtained. A summary of the investigation is given in chapter 3, which is followed by a fuller description of the findings.

Chapter 2

THE PUPILS AND THE TESTS

THE CHOICE OF THE SAMPLE

Five areas were selected by the Committee to provide a cross-section of the various types of community to be found in Scotland. They included a large city, a fairly large county with a mixture of industrial and rural areas, two smaller counties and the industrial section of a large county. They are numbered 1 to 5 in this report in accordance with the Council's policy not to publish data enabling comparisons to be made between particular areas. All pupils in these areas who had attended schools controlled by education authorities, and who had reached the age of 15 between 18 April 1960 and 31 August 1960, formed the group to be studied but a few schools did not take part.

In 1960, the classification of pupils at the transfer stage from primary to secondary education presented few problems, for the distinction was fairly clear-cut between those allocated to a senior secondary course, ie one leading to the award of a certificate after five years, and those allocated to a junior secondary course, ie one of three or four years' duration and not leading to the award of a national certificate. The pupils in this investigation were therefore classified as senior secondary or junior secondary. For most schools identification was easy, but in a few cases special consideration had to be given.

The numbers involved, classified by sex and type of course, are shown in table 1. The number of schools was 97; three senior secondary schools in area 1 were unwilling to provide the necessary facilities.

The differences in the proportions of boys and girls in each area were not significant in the statistical sense ($\chi^2 = 1 \cdot 3$, $P = 0 \cdot 9$), but the differences in the proportions taking senior secondary and junior secondary courses in the five areas were significant $(\chi^2 = 66\cdot2, \ P < 0\cdot01)$. Areas 4 and 5 contained higher proportions of senior secondary pupils than areas 1, 2 and 3. Two large, and one small, senior secondary schools in area 1 declined the invitation to participate. Area 5 contained a

TABLE 1

NUMBERS TAKING 1960 TESTS

	Area					Total	
	1	2	3	4	5		
Girls in JS courses	441	140	70	419	120	1190	1711
Girls in SS courses	151	45	28	233	64	521	
Boys in JS courses	466	148	85	475	88	1262	1836
Boys in SS courses	175	37	23	240	99	574	
Totals	1233	370	206	1367	371	3547	

large senior secondary boys' school which also served other areas outwith its own immediate locality and this explains the very high proportion of senior secondary boys in that area. Area 4 contained a number of fee-paying secondary schools all of whose pupils were classified as senior secondary and this may account for the excess of senior secondary pupils in the area.

THE CONSTRUCTION OF THE TESTS

The aim of the investigation was to measure basic skills in arithmetic and English.

Originally the Committee decided that two tests of three-quarters of an hour in each subject would be necessary so that, allowing for breaks, the total time required for testing would be about four hours.

At this stage also, some consideration was given to the possibility of including an oral test in English. Some members of the Committee felt that the traditional type of English written test was not entirely suitable, since spoken English was used more widely than written English as a means of communication at the present time. A substantial proportion of the community appeared to have little need to retain after leaving school the ability to write or comprehend written English. The difficulties inherent in administering such a test to a widely scattered sample eventually led the Committee to dismiss this possibility.

The advisability of reducing the total testing time to over-come difficulties in administration at the re-test stage soon became apparent. Accordingly, it was decided to curtail the arithmetic test to one paper and the English test to one paper, each requiring about three-quarters of an hour to answer.

The construction of the test papers was remitted to two panels of teachers, one dealing with arithmetic, the other with English. The remit to the panels was to construct test papers which could first be administered to a group of pupils of all grades of ability shortly before they reached school-leaving age and could be applied a year later to the same group for purposes of comparison. The papers had therefore to include questions which could be attempted by the less able pupils as well as questions which would offer a challenge to the average and very able child of nearly 16. In addition it would be necessary to give enough room to show a fall-away in ability at the re-test stage even among the less able.

THE ARITHMETIC TEST

The arithmetic panel decided to produce a test paper in two sections, requiring a total time of fifty minutes.

| Section I | Mechanical Arithmetic | 45 questions requiring a time of 20 minutes |
| Section II | Arithmetical Reasoning | 50 questions requiring a time of 30 minutes |

It was also agreed that half of the items should be reasonably easy, thus providing room for a possible decrease in some pupils' scores and the remaining items should increase in difficulty through the second half thus providing scope for the abler pupils.

Two draft tests were prepared and tried out in a number of schools. The selection of items for the final test paper was based on an item-analysis of the try-out test papers. The actual test used in the investigation can be found at the end of this chapter.

It will be seen that the arithmetical reasoning paper posed problems of a sort that had become traditional in the arithmetic class. Thus it tested arithmetical procedures only a little less stereotyped than the paper in mechanical arithmetic. It did not, therefore, in any way test mathematical understanding or skill. Nevertheless, as was the case with the English tests, the tests were testing in the very field about which complaints had been made. Thus the test is appropriate to the inquiry, but the danger of extrapolating the findings is no less than in the case of the English test.

THE ENGLISH TEST

The remit from the Committee to the English panel recommended that the English tests should include written composition of some kind, spelling, and correct English usage. The Committee was well aware of the difficulties of awarding reliable and valid marks to work of the essay type but felt that a test entirely of the objective type would not be suitable in view of the aims of the investigation.

It was agreed that the test material

1 should indicate something of what the schools had covered in English;
2 should be considered reasonably worth knowing;
3 should not be too easily remembered when the second test was due;
4 should not date, in view of the re-test.

The English panel was not in favour of the inclusion of composition in the English tests on the grounds that it had been found impossible to obtain an objective marking scheme and that the additional time required would make the test too long. Nevertheless the Committee was of the opinion that employers might regard the investigation as having failed in its purpose if composition were excluded. One of the main criticisms of employers was that young employees appeared unable to write English. It was necessary therefore to find a direct measure of writing ability and to convince the general public of its validity. Realising that the layman, unable to appreciate the testing powers of an English test not including composition, might fail to be convinced by its results, the Committee accordingly persisted in its decision to retain composition as part of the test, but did agree to separate composition from the main English paper. In reaching this decision the Committee emphasised its awareness of the difficulties of awarding reliable and valid marks to work of the essay type, and of the need to devise a marking scheme which would be as objective as possible.

Draft tests were prepared and tried out in a number of schools. The selection of items for the final test paper was based on an item analysis of the try-out test-papers. In its final form it contained the following material.

Section I	Spelling (Homonyms)	6 questions
Section II	Punctuation	10 questions
Section III	Spelling	20 questions
Section IV	English Usage	10 questions
Section V	Vocabulary Test	10 questions
Section VI	Vocabulary (Word building by definition)	10 questions

The test is printed in full at the end of this chapter.

It will be noted by the reader that the questions tested only the basic skills of English, those very aspects that were long the subject of so much routine instruction, often at the expense of the acquisition of other, less tangible, skills that in recent years have come to be seen as the pre-requisites of effective writing in English. Nevertheless, it was deficiencies in these same basic skills about which complaints had been made, and it was not therefore unreasonable to use such a test. What must, however, be avoided is any attempt to extrapolate the findings of the inquiry to cover the whole of the skills involved in writing English. The composition test, with all its inherent difficulties of assessment, alone attempted to measure these wider skills.

THE COMPOSITION TEST

The Committee agreed to choose a topic relating to the pupils' lives and interests which would enable the least able pupils to provide sufficient material for assessment. After a try-out of a number of topics the final choice was 'What I think about Jobs'. The time for the composition test was fixed at twenty minutes. To avoid leaving the administration of the test entirely to the individual teacher a set of simply-worded instructions was printed in the composition papers (pp 49 and 50) and a note sent to the teachers inviting their co-operation and indicating that the pupils should be given as little help as possible except in the case of the least able pupils with limited reading ability to whom the teachers might read the instructions.

SCORING OF TESTS

The marking of the English and arithmetic tests was made as objective as possible. For each test, an answer key was drawn up by the appropriate panel, showing the allocation of marks to the individual items and listing the acceptable answers and, where necessary, unacceptable answers. The markers were informed that they must adhere rigidly to the marking scheme outlined in the key. Copies of the keys are shown on pages 51 to 54.

The first set of scripts was marked by the teachers in the schools used in the investigation, and the Council again acknowledges the debt it owes to the Scottish teachers who undertake extra work of this type for the Council on a voluntary basis. The marking was checked in the Council offices by students from a College of Education. At the re-test stage the scripts of pupils still at school were again marked by the teachers concerned. The scripts of pupils who had left school were marked by a retired teacher and members of the Council staff. The marking was checked by Council staff.

The method used to assess the compositions is discussed in detail in Appendix A. Essentially, the method depends on selecting specimen compositions to represent particular levels of achievement. In this case five compositions were selected by three judges following this method. These five compositions were graded A B C D E respectively and copies given to each marker. The marker then compared each essay against the standard essays and graded it accordingly. The marking was carried out by twenty-five Edinburgh teachers following a meeting at which the principles underlying the assessment system were explained to them.

THE SCOTTISH COUNCIL FOR RESEARCH IN EDUCATION

ARITHMETIC

Fill in the following particulars at once:

Your surname ....
        (IN CAPITALS)

Your Christian name(s) ....

Your sex (Boy or Girl) ....

Name of your school...

Class you are in ....

Your age ....

Date of birth ....

Section 1	
Page	Score
2	
3	
4	
5	
6	
7	
Total	
Section 2	
8	
9	
10	
11	
12	
Total	
Grand total	

Read the following carefully:

1 This test is in two sections. There are 6 pages in the first section and 5 pages in the second. Twenty minutes will be allowed for section 1 and thirty minutes for section 2.

2 You may do any working in the space provided.

3 Work as quickly and as carefully as you can. Make any alterations in your answers clearly.

4 No one is expected to do everything. Just do as much as you can. If you cannot do a question do not lose time on it but leave it out and go on to the next.

5 When you are told to do so, turn over to page 2. The instructions at the top of page 2 will be read to you while you follow. You must then start working the test at once.

6 When you have finished one page go on to the next, as far as page 7. Do not turn over to page 8 until you are told.

7 When you are told to stop, stop working at once.

8 Ask no questions at all.

2

SECTION 1

Answer these questions as carefully and as quickly as you can. Be careful to look at the top of each question to see whether it says 'add', 'subtract', 'multiply', 'divide' or gives any other instruction. Do any workings for each in its own space and put the answer in the space provided for it. All vulgar fractions must be expressed in their lowest terms and as mixed numbers where appropriate.

You will have 20 minutes for this section. Now begin.

1 Add

```
1 5 7 2
   5 3
  4 3 7
───────
```

2 Subtract

```
7 4 3
5 9 7
─────

─────
```

3 Multiply

```
5 4 7
  7 3
─────


─────

─────
```

4 Divide

```
  ───────
6 ) 8 2 1 4
```

5 Find the remainder when 82791 is divided by 35.

6 Add

£	s	d
1	3	$4\frac{1}{2}$
3	18	6
2	13	$10\frac{1}{2}$
	9	$8\frac{1}{2}$

£   :   :

7 Subtract   3s $10\frac{1}{2}$d from 10s.

s   d

8 Change 340 pence to £ s d.

£   :   :

GO STRAIGHT ON TO NEXT PAGE

3

9 Multiply

£	s	d
2	16	4
		8

£ : :

10 Divide

£	s	d

12) 8 4   2   6

11 Subtract

yd	ft	in
45	2	7
17	2	9

12 Multiply

st	lb	oz
3	9	7
		7

13 Divide

gal	qt	pt

8) 2 5   0   0

14 Divide

cwt	st	lb

6) 2 8   7   6

15 $\frac{3}{8}+\frac{5}{16}+\frac{1}{2}$

16 $4\frac{3}{5}-2\frac{14}{15}$

GO STRAIGHT ON TO NEXT PAGE

4

17 $3\frac{1}{7} \times 2\frac{6}{11}$ **18** $4\frac{1}{6} \div 2\frac{11}{12}$

19 Simplify $\dfrac{56 \times 14 \times 27}{32 \times 18 \times 49}$ **20 Add**   57·32, 8·59, 42 and 5·4

21 Subtract   2·83 from 10·6   **22 Multiply** $\begin{array}{r} 1\,7 \cdot 5 \\ 2 \cdot 5 \\ \hline \\ \hline \\ \hline \end{array}$

23 Divide   18·3 by 0·6   **24 Simplify** $\dfrac{2\cdot1 \times 0\cdot08}{0\cdot3 \times 0\cdot4}$

GO STRAIGHT ON TO NEXT PAGE

5

25 Simplify $\dfrac{3 \cdot 3 \times 6 \cdot 9 \times 0 \cdot 125}{2 \cdot 3 \times 0 \cdot 55 \times 0 \cdot 15}$ **26**   Change 3 hr 50 min to seconds.

seconds

27 Change $72\frac{3}{25}$ to a decimal.   **28** Express 45 per cent as a vulgar fraction in its lowest terms.

29 What fraction of £1 2s 6d is 16s 10½d ?

30 Find the average of 87, 35, 52, 62 and 49.   **31** What is the cost of 61 articles at 2s 6d per dozen ?

s   d

GO STRAIGHT ON TO NEXT PAGE

6

32 What is the cost of 7 oz of tea at 6s 8d per lb ?

33 What is the cost of 3 gross of pencils at 1½d each ?

s   d

£   :   :

34 What is the cost of 2 ft 9 in of material at 5s 4d per foot ?

35 What is the cost of 2 tons of coal at 8s 6d per cwt ?

s   d

£   :   :

36 What percentage of 5080 is 3810 ?

37 Express 16s as a percentage of £1.

38 What is 12½ per cent of 6 tons ?

39 Find 8⅓ per cent of £20 16s.

cwt

£   :   :

GO STRAIGHT ON TO NEXT PAGE

40 Express 3s 9½d as a decimal of 5s 5d.

41 Express 15s 9d as a decimal of £1 to four decimal places.

42 Change £1·134 to £ s d to the nearest penny.

43 If log 1·205=0·0809, what is log 120·5 ?

£   :   :

44   log 3=0·4771
log 5=0·6990
What is log 15 ?

45 If log 2=0·3010, what is log 8 ?

END OF SECTION 1

**LOOK OVER YOUR WORK IN SECTION 1 UNTIL TIME IS UP
DO NOT TURN OVER TO PAGE 8 UNTIL YOU ARE TOLD**

8

SECTION 2

Answer these questions as quickly and as carefully as you can. If you cannot do a question leave it out and go on to the next. The questions need not be worked mentally. Do any working in the space at the left and put your answer in the place provided at the right. Vulgar fractions must be expressed in their lowest terms and as mixed numbers where appropriate. Answers must be given in the units indicated.

You will have 30 minutes for this section.

Working

1 After a woman had spent 5s 4½d, a shopkeeper gave her 2s 1½d change. How much had she given the shopkeeper ?

.................s   ....d

2 How far will a cyclist travel in 3 hours cycling at 10½ miles per hour ?

.....................miles

3 How many 4-oz packets of tea can be made from 4½ lb ?

.....................packets

4 A train was due to arrive at 1.50 pm. It was 37 minutes late. At what time did it arrive ?

.....................pm

5 What is the cost of 493 articles at 6s 8d each ?

£.......... : .... : ....

6 In 1950 a boy was two years old. In what year was he three times as old ?

....

7 A school has £5 5s 0d to spend on prizes. How many books at 7s 6d each can be bought ?

.................books

8 A lorry weighs 2 tons 5 cwt empty and 7 tons 3 cwt full of coal. What weight of coal does it hold ?

..........tons   ....cwt

GO STRAIGHT ON TO NEXT PAGE

Working

9 Find the cost of 80 tables at £4 17s 6d each.

£....................

10 Fencing posts are placed 7 ft apart. What is the distance between the first post and the tenth post ?

....................ft

11 A workman's bus takes 35 minutes to get him to work. He arrived one morning at the stop at 7.19 am and had to wait 11 minutes before the bus came. When did he arrive at work ?

....................am

12 What is the area in sq yd of a rectangular plot 36 ft long and 24 ft broad ?

....................sq yd

13 Coal is sold in tubs holding $1\frac{1}{4}$ cwt. How many tubs of coal should I order to get 1 ton ?

....................tubs

14 A rectangular lawn measuring 5 yd by 6 yd is to be sown at a cost of 9d per sq yd. What is the total cost?

£.......... : .... : ....

15 If 24 books cost £16 what is the cost of 39 ?

£....................

16 A soldier's pace is 30 inches. He walks at the rate of 120 paces a minute. How many yards does he walk in a minute ?

....................yd

17 What is the total postage on 10 letters (postage 3d each), 7 postcards (postage $2\frac{1}{2}$d each) and 5 birthday cards (postage 2d each) ?

..........s ....d

GO STRAIGHT ON TO NEXT PAGE

10

Working

18 A joiner's wage is 4s 4½d an hour and an apprentice's 3s 1½d an hour. What is the total cost of a job which occupies them 7 hours if material costs £1 2s 6d ?

£............ : .... : ....

19 Letter postage is 3d for the first oz and 1½d for each additional oz or part of an oz. What is the postage for a letter weighing 3½ oz ?

......................d

20 A car covers a distance of 150 miles in 4 hours. What is its average speed in miles per hour ?

......................mph

21 If the perimeter of a square is 64 feet, what is its area ?

......................sq ft

22 If 15 men do a piece of work in 22 days, how long should 20 men take ?

......................days

23 On weekdays a man works from 8 am to 5 pm with ¾ of an hour off for dinner. How many hours per week does he work in a 5-day week ?

......................hr

24 What is the cost of a carpet 12 ft by 9 ft at £1 17s 6d per sq yd ?

£............ : .... : ....

25 £4 10s is divided between John and Tom so that for every 2s 6d John receives Tom will receive 2s. How much will John receive ?

£............ : .... : ....

26 Two workmen together are paid £1 10s. If Smith works 3½ hours on the job and Jones 1½ hours, how much does Jones get ?

......................s

GO STRAIGHT ON TO NEXT PAGE

11

Working

27 You can buy a bicycle for £19 10s or pay £1 10s down and then 17s 6d a month for 2 years. How much more does the bicycle cost by the second method ?

£....................

28 A railway wagon when empty weighs 5 tons, when full of coal 15 tons 10 cwt. What should it weigh when half-full of coal ?

...........tons ....cwt

29 A bottle holds 1¼ pints. How many such bottles can be filled from a 5-gallon drum ?

....................bottles

30 A lace border 6 inches wide is added to a table cloth 6 ft by 4 ft. What is the area of the border ?

....................sq ft

31 Two parents and three children spent 15s 9d on rail fares. If the children all pay half-fare, what is the adult fare for the journey ?

...........s ....d

32 From the first rung to the tenth rung of a ladder the distance is 11 ft 3 in. If the rungs are equally spaced, what is the distance between two rungs ?

.................ft ....in

33 A train travels 87 miles in 90 minutes. How far does it travel in 1 hour ?

.................miles

34 A wagon-load of coal provides coal for 32 days for a furnace burning 42 lb of coal a day. How long would a wagon-load last if the furnace used 56 lb a day ?

....................days

35 A box containing 35 tins of fruit weighs 58 lb. When 20 tins are removed it weighs 28 lb. What is the weight of the empty box ?

.................lb

GO STRAIGHT ON TO NEXT PAGE

12

Working

36 A box of chocolates weighs 1 lb 5 oz. The chocolates weigh 13 oz more than the box. What is the weight of the chocolates ?

.............lb ....oz

37 Find the circumference of a circle, radius $4\frac{1}{5}$ in $(\pi = \frac{22}{7})$.

.......................in

38 Find the simple interest on £120 for $2\frac{1}{2}$ years at 3 per cent per annum.

£.......................

39 If 1350 francs are equivalent to £1 find the value in English money of 4320 francs.

£............ : .... : ....

40 A rectangular courtyard 14 ft by 8 ft is to be covered with square tiles of side 6 in. How many are required ?

.......................tiles

41 A book was sold for 12s 6d at a profit of 2s 6d. What is the rate of profit per cent ?

.......................per cent

42 If Local Rates are fixed at 18s 9d in the £, what should be paid by a householder whose house is assessed at £36 ?

£............ : .... : ....

43 Three people share £527 8s 6d in the ratios of 1 : 2 : 3. Find the smallest share.

£............ : .... : ....

44 $2\frac{1}{2}$ per cent of the contents are lost from a 20-gallon drum of oil. How many pints are left ?

.......................pints

45 If £1 is worth 2·8 dollars what is the value of 343 dollars in £ s d ?

£............ : .... : ....

GO STRAIGHT ON TO NEXT PAGE

13

Working

46 Mon 437 ⎫
   Tues 416 ⎪ These were the daily attendances in a
   Wed — ⎬ school. The average for the 5 days was 422.
   Thur 425 ⎪ What was the attendance on Wednesday ?
   Fri 408 ⎭

....

47 An angler caught 1 fish weighing $1\frac{1}{2}$ lb, 2 weighing $1\frac{1}{4}$ lb each, 3 weighing 1 lb each, 2 weighing $\frac{3}{4}$ lb each and 1 weighing $\frac{1}{2}$ lb. What was the average weight per fish ?

.......................lb

48 A square classroom has an area of 625 sq ft. What is the length of a side ?

.......................ft

49 An aeroplane flew 448 miles in 42 minutes. Calculate its average speed in miles per hour.

.......................mph

50 A pupil's marks in two papers were 95 out of 125 and 69 out of 80. What percentage of the total marks did he obtain ?

.......................per cent

END OF SECTION 2

LOOK OVER YOUR WORK IN SECTION 2 UNTIL TIME IS UP

DO NOT GO BACK TO SECTION 1

THE SCOTTISH COUNCIL FOR RESEARCH IN EDUCATION

ENGLISH

Section	Score
1	
2	
3	
4	
5	
6	
Total	

Fill in the following particulars at once:

Your surname..
     (IN CAPITALS)

Your Christian name(s)...

....

Your sex (Boy or Girl) ....

Name of your school..

Class you are in .... Your age.............................

Date of birth ....

Read the following carefully:

1 The time allowed for this test is 40 minutes.

2 <u>Work as quickly and as carefully as you can.</u> Make any alterations in your answer <u>clearly.</u>

3 You may not be able to do everything. Just do as much as you can. If you cannot do a question do not lose time on it but leave it out and go on to the next.

4 When you are told to do so turn over to page 2, and start work on the test. The instructions for each section are given at the beginning of the section.

5 When you are told to stop, <u>stop working at once.</u>

6 Ask no questions at all.

2

SECTION 1

Underline the correct word within the brackets.

1 The coat is (hers, her's, hers').

2 The footballers were angry when (there, their, they're) train was late.

3 '(Who's, Whose) interested in gliding?' asked the instructor. 'I know a farmer (who's, whose) field would suit us.'

4 '(Its, It's) clear,' said Tom, 'that the bird has broken (its, it's) wing.'

5 They started (of, off) on their trek at break (of, off) day.

6 The (too, two, to) boys found (too, to, two) their dismay they had allowed the boat to drift (to, two, too) far.

SECTION 2

In these sentences some punctuation marks have been left out.
Put them in at the correct places on your paper.

1 The boy rang the door bell nobody came.

2 'Where are you going, Bob' asked Tom.

3 What a lovely scene I must photograph it.

4 The customer bought tea coffee and sugar.

5 'Can you tell me,' asked the driver, where South Street is ?'

6 I am going to St Marys.

7 Watt a native of Greenock invented a steam engine.

8 You cant go in there.

9 His favourite song was The Road to the Isles.

10 Please arrange for supplies of the following equipment ropes, ice-axes, goggles and crampons.

3

SECTION 3

Write in full, **in the spaces provided at the end of the letter,** *the words numbered in the following letter.*

7 Kirk Lane,

Troytown.

(1) Sat   day, 7th (2) Feb   ry, 1959.

Dear Mr Brown,

I shall be (3) ind   ted to you if you will make the (4) nec   sary arrange-ments for my two (5) n   ces to see the snapshots of your (6) Med   nean holiday. I have (7) h   d you are a (8) sk   f   l photographer. No doubt you have (9) ben   t   d by (10) pos   sing (11) ac   m   dation at home where you may (12) practi   e. They will count it a great (13) priv   ge to see the results of your own (14) ind   p   nt effort.

No doubt they will need to (15) ex   r   ise patience until you (16) suc   d in fixing a date, but I assure they will be (17) dis   pointed if you find it (18) inconv   n   t to arrange this (19) b   s   ness.

Yours (20) sin   ly,

Tom Green.

(1) ....   (8) ....   (15) ....

(2) ....   (9) ....   (16) ....

(3) ....   (10) ....   (17) ....

(4) ....   (11) ....   (18) ....

(5) ....   (12) ....   (19) ....

(6) ....   (13) ....   (20) ....

(7) ....   (14) ....

4

SECTION 4

Underline **one** *word wrongly used in each of the five sentences below and write the correct word in the space provided.*

1 The man admits that he done it. ....

2 The prizes are to be given to you and I. ....

3 Your house is quite different than mine. ....

4 Do not waste your time like your brother does. ....

5 Somebody told me; I forget whom it was. ....

Rewrite the following in correct English.

6 Coming home late, the house was locked up.

....

7 I think yours and my dress are both suitable.

....

8 One may do as he likes in his own house.

....

9 It is dangerous travelling in that country.

....

10 The committee requests subscriptions to be paid to the treasurer.

....

5

SECTION 5

Underline the correct meaning of the words printed in capitals.

ORIENTAL *means*   from the West; from the East; Chinese; foreign; oriel.

CHRONIC *means*   acute; dangerous; lasting; boring; virulent.

RECTIFY *means*   rule; measure; alter; erect; make right.

CREDIBLE *means*   truthful; likely; attentive; believable; amazing.

RELUCTANT *means*   relative; unavailing; unwilling; uncertain; redundant.

PENSIVE *means*   timid; considerate; thoughtless; thoughtful; cheap.

AGILITY *means*   nimbleness; bravery; speed; muscular; skill.

ASSENT *means*   amount; agree; climb; verify; demur.

FURTIVE *means*   stealthy; woolly; fertile; guilty; hostile.

DILIGENT *means*   indolent; penniless; clever; industrial; industrious.

SECTION 6

1 *Write down in the space provided* **a word ending in** ....**fy** *which has the same meaning as these phrases:*

   (*a*) to make easier ....

   (*b*) to make something appear bigger ....

2 *Write down in the space provided* **a word ending in** ....**ise** *which has the same meaning as these phrases:*

   (*a*) to show a fellow feeling for someone ....

   (*b*) to take care not to overspend ....

3 *Write down in the space provided* **a word ending in** ....**ate** *which has the same meaning as these phrases:*

   (*a*) to follow closely someone's example...

   (*b*) to be ready beforehand for some expected event ....

   (*c*) to increase the speed of a mechanism ....

   (*d*) to implore someone to grant your request ....

   (*e*) to reduce the severity of a punishment ....

   (*f*) to reduce the severity of pain or suffering ....

THE SCOTTISH COUNCIL FOR RESEARCH IN EDUCATION

COMPOSITION

Fill in the following particulars:

Your surname...
(IN CAPITALS)
Your Christian name(s)..

Name of your school..

You will be given 20 minutes for this paper.

1 If you intend to leave school soon, state briefly why you wish to leave.
If you intend to stay on at school, leave this part blank.

....

....

2 State briefly what kind of job you would like to have when you are grown-up.

....

....

What I think about Jobs

Write an essay—some people call it a composition—on this title—'What I think about Jobs'. You will not be told what to write or how to write it or how to spell any words. Think about it for a minute or so and then begin.

CONTINUE ON OTHER SIDE

PoL/C 1960
4

THE SCOTTISH COUNCIL FOR RESEARCH IN EDUCATION

COMPOSITION

Fill in the following particulars:

Your name ....

Name of your school or former school ....

You will be given 20 minutes for this paper.

What I think about Jobs

Write an essay—some people call it a composition—on this title—'What I think about Jobs'. You will not be told what to write or how to write it or how to spell any words. Think about it for a minute or so and then begin.

CONTINUE ON OTHER SIDE

PoL/C 1961

THE SCOTTISH COUNCIL FOR RESEARCH IN EDUCATION

Answer Key for Arithmetic Test

One mark should be awarded for each item correctly answered. Answers which are not given in the key should not be accepted, but if the teacher feels that an alternative answer is acceptable a note to that effect should be entered on the front of the booklet.

SECTION 1

page 2

1 2062
2 146
3 39931
4 1369
5 16
6 £8 5s 5½d
7 6s 1½d
8 £1 8s 4d

page 3

9 £22 10s 8d
10 £7 0s 2½d
11 27 yd 2 ft 10 in
12 25 st 10 lb 1 oz
13 3 gal 0 qt 1 pt
14 4 cwt 6 st 8 lb
15 $1\frac{3}{16}$
16 $1\frac{2}{3}$

page 4

17 8
18 $1\frac{3}{7}$
19 $\frac{3}{4}$
20 113·31
21 7·77
22 43·75
23 30·5
24 1·4 or $1\frac{2}{5}$

page 5

25 15
26 13,800 sec
27 72·12
28 $\frac{9}{20}$
29 $\frac{3}{4}$ or 0·75
30 57
31 12s 8½d

page 6

32 2s 11d
33 £2 14s 0d
34 14s 8d
35 £17
36 75%
37 80%
38 15 cwt
39 £1 14s 8d

page 7

40 0·7
41 0·7875
42 £1 2s 8d
43 2·0809
44 1·1761
45 0·9030

SECTION 2

page 8

1 7s 6d
2 31½ miles
3 18 packets
4 2·27 pm
5 £164 6s 8d
6 1954
7 14 books
8 4 tons 18 cwt

page 9

9 £390
10 63 ft
11 8·05 or 8·5 am
12 96 sq yd
13 16 tubs
14 £1 2s 6d
15 £26
16 100 yards
17 4s 9½d

page 10

18 £3 15s 0d
19 7½d
20 37½ mph
21 256 sq ft
22 16½ days
23 41¼ hr
24 £22 10s 0d
25 £2 10s 0d
26 9s 0d

page 11

27 £3
28 10 ton 5 cwt
29 32 bottles
30 11 sq ft
31 4s 6d
32 1 ft 3 in
33 58 miles
34 24 days
35 5½ lb

page 12

36 1 lb 1 oz
37 26⅖ in
38 £9
39 £3 4s 0d
40 448 tiles
41 25%
42 £33 15s 0d
43 £87 18s 1d
44 156 pints
45 £122 10s 0d

page 13

46 424
47 1 lb
48 25 ft
49 640 mph
50 80%

THE SCOTTISH COUNCIL FOR RESEARCH IN EDUCATION

Marking Key for English Test

SECTION 1   *One* mark for each *completely* correct answer to a question.   No part marks to be given.

1   hers
2   their
3   Who's; whose
4   It's; its
5   off; of
6   two; to; too

(6 marks)

SECTION 2   *One* mark for each *completely* correct answer

1   bell; nobody *or* bell.   Nobody
2   Bob?'
3   scene! I
4   tea, coffee
5   driver, 'where
6   Mary's
5   Watt, a native of Greenock,
8   can't
9   'The Road to the Isles'
10   equipment: ropes, *or* equipment—ropes

(10 marks)

SECTION 3   *One* mark for each correct answer

1	Saturday	8	skilful	15	exercise
2	February	9	benefited	16	succeed
3	indebted	10	possessing	17	disappointed
4	necessary	11	accommodation	18	inconvenient
5	nieces	12	practise	19	business
6	Mediterranean	13	privilege	20	sincerely
7	heard	14	independent		

(20 marks)

SECTION 4, Items 1–5   *One* mark for each correct answer.   If correction is clear, award mark even if underlining is badly done or omitted.

1   Underline 'done';   write 'did'
2   Underline 'I';   write 'me'
3   Underline 'than';   write 'from'
4   Underline 'like';   write 'as'
5   Underline 'whom';   write 'who'

(5 marks)

SECTION 4, Items 6–10   *One* mark for any correct sentence which eliminates the grammatical error. The errors in these sentences are as follows:

Sentence 6   Misrelated Participle
         7   Use of possessive pronoun instead of possessive case of personal pronoun
         8   Inconsistency of use of pronoun
         9   Misuse of verbal noun
        10   Confusion of constructions

(5 marks)

SECTION 5   *One* mark for each correct answer

1	from the East	6	thoughtful
2	lasting	7	nimbleness
3	make right	8	agree
4	believable	9	stealthy
5	unwilling	10	industrious

(10 marks)

SECTION 6   Award 2 marks if correct word is given, correctly spelt; award 1 mark if correct word is given, but wrongly spelt.

1 (*a*) simplify
  (*b*) magnify
2 (*a*) sympathise
  (*b*) economise
3 (*a*) imitate
  (*b*) anticipate
  (*c*) accelerate
  (*d*) supplicate
  (*e*) mitigate
  (*f*) alleviate *or* palliate

(20 marks)

Total—76 marks

Chapter 3

SUMMARY OF THE INVESTIGATION

The first testing took place in May 1960 in the five selected areas, and a total of 3547 pupils in 97 schools returned scripts. The re-test was fixed for March 1961 rather than May 1961 since young people attending further education evening classes would still be available then. It was expected that a major difficulty in the experiment would be making contact with the young people at the re-test stage.

The young people concerned in the first stage of the investigation reached the age of 15 between 18 April and 31 August 1960 and were therefore free from the obligation to attend school after the summer vacation of 1960. They could be divided into the following seven categories according to their expected location in March 1961, the expected proportions being based on national data for previous years.

(*a*) those still in attendance at school—25 per cent

(*b*) those in some form of full-time further education at a technical college or similar institution—5 per cent

(*c*) those attending day-release classes at a further education centre—5 per cent

(*d*) those attending a further education centre of some type voluntarily in the evenings only—25 per cent

(*e*) those working for the larger employers who conduct their own apprenticeship training schemes—unknown

(*f*) those at work but not attending any further education classes—unknown

(*g*) those unemployed—unknown

The Committee considered that it would be possible to arrange for the re-testing of categories (*a*) to (*e*), those of (*f*) employed by firms willing to co-operate, and those of (*g*), through headmasters, principals of further education colleges and evening class centres, personnel managers, and youth employment officers. For categories (*a*) to (*d*), arrangements were made to have the re-test carried out in the school, or further education centre. For categories (*e*) and (*f*), employers in larger firms were asked to give facilities for the test to be held during working hours. The employers in smaller firms were asked to release the young people concerned during working hours to attend for testing at a given centre. For those not covered by these arrangements, testing was carried out at centres in the evening and the young person was encouraged to attend.

The procedure adopted in tracing and classifying the young people under headings (*a*) to (*g*) was as follows:

1 In October 1960 each school in the five selected areas was sent a list of the names of the young people who sat the first test in that school and the headteacher was asked to mark the names of those who had left school, distinguishing those who had entered full-time education elsewhere.

2 On receipt of these lists the names of the leavers were sent to the principal of the local technical college or evening class centre, who was asked if the young person had enrolled and, if so, what classes were being attended.

3 Where the employer was known, a letter was sent asking whether the firm had its own training scheme for young people and also whether it would co-operate by providing facilities for testing on its own premises or alternatively by releasing the young employee to attend at the appropriate testing centre. The same letter was sent to the major employers in the five areas in an endeavour to inform as many as possible of the employers of the young people concerned.

4 The youth employment officers of the areas concerned were consulted regarding possible arrangements for testing the young people not attending classes.

5 Where contact could not be made with the young person by any of the preceding methods a personal letter was sent to him explaining the need for the follow-up and asking him to attend at the appropriate centre. In addition, use was made of voluntary helpers. One hundred and sixty-one students at colleges of education visited over a thousand (1047) young

people at their homes, in order to explain the purpose of the re-test and to encourage them to attend for re-testing.

The co-operation given by headteachers, by principals of technical colleges and further education centres and by youth employment officers was excellent although the last group were restricted by the rules of the Service, which prohibited the divulging of the names of employers to bodies such as the Council. On the other hand, some of the youth employment officers organised and supervised testing sessions. As will be

TABLE 2

EMPLOYERS' RESPONSE TO LETTERS INVITING CO-OPERATION

Area	No of letters despatched	No of replies	Category of reply			
			(a)	(b)	(c)	(d)
1	389	131	7	22	12	90
2	160	42	5	13	3	21
3	57	17	1	10	3	3
4	542	164	11	92	22	39
5	117	27	4	15	5	3
Totals	1265	381	28	152	45	156

Coding (a) Employer willing to test on own premises
 (b) Employer willing to release for testing
 (c) Employer willing to encourage to attend at a testing centre in employees' own time
 (d) Employer had no employees in the age-group concerned

seen from table 2 the co-operation of employers was very mixed. Some were most co-operative, others were not. Only 30 per cent replied to the Council's letter of inquiry. An analysis of the data shows no significant differences among the five areas in the responses of employers.

Of the 3547 young people who took the tests in 1960, only 1798 or 51 per cent took the tests again in 1961. If the 51 per cent could have been regarded as a representative sample of the original group it would have been possible to continue the investigation on the lines originally laid down. But a preliminary examination showed that the 51 per cent could not be so regarded. Of the young people who had continued at school, 84 per cent were re-tested, and those attending further education centres provided a 57 per cent response. Of those who had left school and were not enrolled in any form of further education, only 24 per cent attended for the second set of tests and questionnaires. The 1961 group could not be considered as representative of the 1960 group.

In view of these findings the Committee decided that from the wealth of data at its disposal it should present a picture of the basic attainments of those young people who reached the age of 15 in the summer of 1960, showing (*a*) what they knew at 15; (*b*) what they did between the ages of 15 and 16; and (*c*) what they retained after an interval of nearly a year. These findings are presented in chapters 5 to 8, but these chapters are preceded by a description in chapter 4 of the additional information which the Committee acquired about these young people.

Chapter 4

BACKGROUND MATERIAL

At the administration of the first set of tests each school was asked to complete a sociological schedule for each pupil. The schedule provided the following information: the pupil's home address, position in the family and size of family, date of birth and father's occupation. The headmaster was also asked to state what he considered to be the reason for the pupil's leaving school.

As part of the composition test paper the pupil was asked to give his reason for leaving school and the type of job he preferred to be in, when grown-up.

At the re-test stage each member of the group was asked to complete a questionnaire which provided the following additional information:

> new address if any change had been made
> present job and duration of employment
> job preferred when 21
> mother's occupation (if working)
> further education courses attended
> spare-time leisure activities
> membership of youth organisations
> names of newspapers and last book read

The question of social background was considered and it was agreed by the Committee that the rateable value of the house occupied would give a fair indication of socio-economic circumstances.

Copies of the schedule and questionnaire complete this chapter. The coding of the information was a laborious task. As many of the items were of the open-ended type, the choice of a suitable coding scheme was of great importance if information was not to be lost. The coding schemes adopted and the difficulties facing the Committee and the coders are discussed in the appropriate sections of chapters 6 and 7.

THE SCOTTISH COUNCIL FOR RESEARCH IN EDUCATION

SOCIOLOGICAL SCHEDULE

This schedule should be completed by the Headmaster, Careers Master or other member of staff, but not by the pupil.   It should be returned along with the completed tests to the Research Council at 46 Moray Place, Edinburgh 3.

1 Name of pupil ....

2 Home address ....

....

3 Date of birth..

4 Occupation of father or guardian ....
(See Note 1 on facing page)

5 Position in family and size of family...
(See Note 2 on facing page)

6 Why is this pupil leaving school? ....
(To be completed where applicable)
(See Note 3 on facing page)

....

....

7

8

9

10

NOTES

1 Occupation of father or guardian

Please make the reply to this question as specific as possible, as the information is to be used to classify the pupils in groups, according to father's occupation. Answers such as 'engineer', 'civil servant', 'local government employee' are too vague to yield any useful information: the answers in these cases should define the type of engineer, the rank of civil servant, or the type of work done in the local government service.

2 Position in family and size of family

This should be expressed in the form of a fraction, eg, $\frac{1}{1}$ is an only child; $\frac{2}{3}$ is the middle child of three; $\frac{7}{7}$ is the youngest child of seven. Only full brothers and sisters now alive should be included.

3 Reason for leaving school

Only a brief statement need be given; it should express the school's estimate of the real reason for the pupil's leaving school.

4 Questions 7, 8, 9 and 10

These spaces are provided for items for which the school is not asked to supply information.

This schedule was completed by

Name ....

School ....

THE SCOTTISH COUNCIL FOR RESEARCH IN EDUCATION

Last summer you sat two tests and wrote a short composition for the Research Council. Those studying the results would now like you to answer the following questions. Your answers will not be made known separately to anyone, but will be combined with those of others to give a general picture.

Your Name...

Your Address ....

Work   1 What is your present job? ....

        2 State briefly what you do...

        ....

        3 How long have you had your job? ....

        4 What job would you like to have by the time you are 21? ....

        ....

        5 If your mother works, what is her job? ....

Study   6 If you attended night school during the winter, what were your main subjects? ....

        7 On how many nights in the week did you attend? ....

        8 Do you attend day release classes? ....

Leisure   9 What do you do in your spare time? ....

        ....

     10 Give the name of any youth organisation of which you are a member

        ....

     11 Which newspapers do you read regularly?.......................................

        ....

     12 Do you borrow books from the library?..

     13 What was the last book you read? ....

        ....

Chapter 5

WHAT THE YOUNG PEOPLE KNEW
AT THE AGE OF 15

INTRODUCTION

Since the investigation had its origins in statements that some young people leaving school were ill-equipped in the basic skills, the tests were restricted to those of English and arithmetic. They were, in fact, applied to pupils following a wide variety of courses and covering the whole range of ability in the secondary school. The investigation makes no profession of assessing or even sampling the whole field of secondary school subjects but is restricted to the basic skills of English and arithmetic.

This chapter gives an analysis of the scores made by the young people at the first testing in 1960. The relations of these scores to variables such as sex, father's occupation, type of course followed at school and reasons given for leaving school are studied in chapter 6.

The reader is reminded that the group of young people cannot be regarded as a *random* sample of all Scottish young people of the same age. The areas from which they were drawn were a *judgment* sample, not a random sample, of all areas in Scotland. It is therefore not possible to use the statistical methods applicable to simple random sampling or to cluster sampling. At the same time the areas were chosen to include most of the various types in Scotland with the exception of the sparsely populated Highland area and the conclusions are probably applicable to the greater part of Scotland as it was in 1960.

There is a similar sampling situation with regard to the items of the test. Any test can contain only a sample of the very large number of items that can be considered as worthy of inclusion. The selection of the items for the test was a judgment sampling, supported as it was by try-outs of the items and analysis of the responses.

DISTRIBUTION OF TOTAL SCORES IN ARITHMETIC

The distribution of scores on the arithmetic test is shown in figure 1. The scores of the 3465 pupils who took the test have been grouped in class intervals of five. The table of frequencies from which the diagram was constructed is given in Appendix E, table 86. The maximum possible score on the test was 95, which no one achieved. The average score on the test was 32·35.

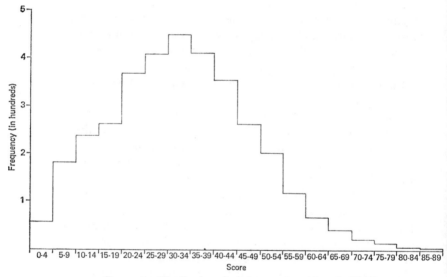

FIGURE 1   Distribution of total scores in arithmetic (1960)

DISTRIBUTION OF SCORES IN MECHANICAL ARITHMETIC

Figure 2 shows the distribution of scores in this section of the arithmetic test. Again the scores of the 3468 pupils who sat the test have been grouped in class intervals of five. The maximum possible score was 45. The average score was 16·7.

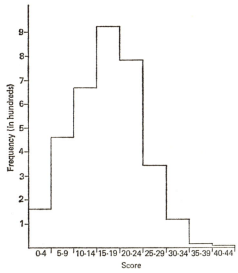

FIGURE 2   Distribution of scores in mechanical arithmetic (1960)

DISTRIBUTION OF SCORES IN ARITHMETICAL REASONING

Similarly, figure 3 shows the distribution of scores on this section of the arithmetic test in which the maximum possible score was 50. The average score on this section of the test was 15·6.

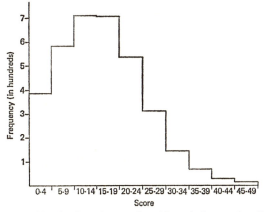

FIGURE 3   Distribution of scores in arithmetical reasoning (1960)

5

From the point of view of the test construction, the arithmetic test as a whole was satisfactory at this stage. It gave scope for the bright pupil to show his proficiency and also discriminated among the less able. A possible criticism of the arithmetical reasoning test is that it did not allow sufficient scope for the less able pupil in that there was considerable bunching of the scores in the 0–4 range.

MEDIANS AND QUARTILES FOR THE ARITHMETIC TESTS

To facilitate description of the pupils' performance, use has been made of the 'median', the 'quartile' and the 'percentile' scores. The 'median score' can be thought of as the score made by the middle pupil when the scores are arranged in order of merit. It corresponds closely to the average score, though it may differ slightly from it. The 'lower quartile score' (Q1) is that score which separates the lowest quarter of the pupils from the rest; the 'upper quartile score' (Q3) is that which separates the top quarter from the rest.

'Percentile scores' are defined in similar fashion by dividing the distribution of pupils' scores into a hundred parts. The 10th percentile (P10) divides the lowest 10 per cent of the pupils from the remainder; the 60th percentile (P60) separates the lower 60 per cent of the pupils from the upper 40 per cent. The lower quartile score (Q1) therefore corresponds to the 25th percentile, the median score corresponds to the 50th percentile, while the upper quartile score (Q3) corresponds to the 75th percentile.

The quartile and percentile scores usually contain fractions of a mark since it is unusual for an integral percentage of a group to be above or below a particular integral score. For example, if 22·5 per cent of the group are below 11 and 23·5 per cent below 12, then the 23rd percentile (P23) is half-way between 11 and 12 and is defined as 11·5.

In this chapter, the median score has been taken as typical of the average pupil, the lower quartile score has been taken as typical of the below average or less able pupil, and the upper quartile score as typical of the above average or abler pupil.

Table 3 gives these scores for both sections of the arithmetic test and for the complete test. The percentile appropriate to each of the possible scores in the test is given in Appendix E, table 89.

TABLE 3

QUARTILE AND MEDIAN SCORES FOR ARITHMETIC TEST

	Q1	Median	Q3	Maximum possible mark
Mechanical arithmetic	11·4	16·9	22·0	45
Arithmetical reasoning	8·6	14·9	21·6	50
Complete test	21·2	32·1	42·4	95

The sum of the quartile scores for both parts of the test does not equal the quartile score for the test taken as a whole, since the poorest quarter in the mechanical arithmetic section is not necessarily the lowest quarter in the arithmetical reasoning section of the test.

PERFORMANCE ON THE VARIOUS ITEMS OF THE ARITHMETIC TESTS

There will be less interest in the actual marks than in what they represent in the way of attainments. One way of presenting this information is in the form of tables called answer patterns, showing for each item how many of the pupils gave the correct response, how many gave the wrong response and how many did not attempt the item. Since experience has shown that a sufficiently large random sample of scripts yields representative results, such answer patterns have been prepared from a sample of 205 sets of scripts (106 boys and 99 girls) and are given in Appendix E, table 90.

From them the reader can assess the difficulty of each item and can also observe the frequency with which each item was attempted in each test.

Since tables of figures sometimes do not show trends clearly, the answer patterns are presented in diagrammatic form in figures 4 and 5.

PERFORMANCE OF TYPICAL PUPILS

The answer patterns referred to in the previous section give a picture of the average performance of the whole group.

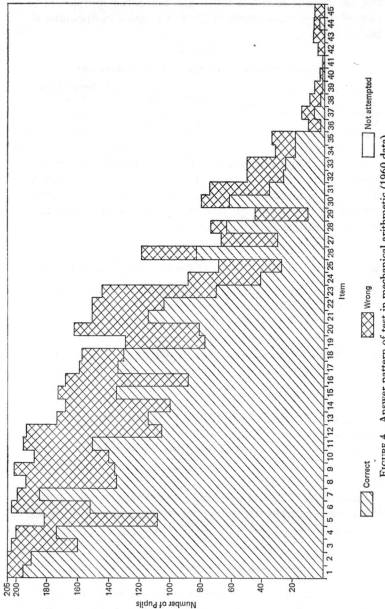

FIGURE 4   Answer pattern of test in mechanical arithmetic (1960 data)

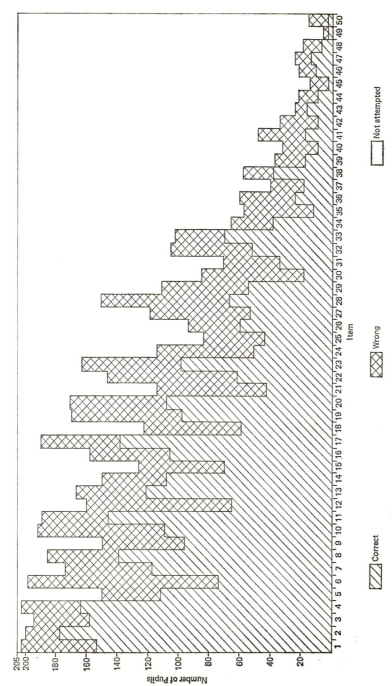

FIGURE 5   Answer pattern of test in arithmetical reasoning (1960 data)

Parents, teachers and employers will also be interested in the performance of pupils at other levels, and answer patterns were therefore prepared for pupils at the 95th, 90th, 75th, 50th, and 25th percentile levels. At the first two levels the number of scripts available was limited and only 11 were used at the P95

TABLE 4

RESPONSES TO ITEMS OF ARITHMETIC TESTS BY PUPILS AT
DIFFERENT LEVELS OF TOTAL SCORE

Level and score	Section of test	Items answered correctly	Items answered wrongly	Items not attempted	Items not classified
P95	Mechanical	1–28, 30–32 **59**	**13**	35–45 **23**	29, 33, 34
(59)	Reasoning	1–17, 19–34, 38	18, 37	43–50	35, 36, 39–42
P90	Mechanical	1–24, 26–28 **54**	25 **13**	29–45 **28**	
(54)	Reasoning	1–29, 32–34	30, 36	31, 35, 38, 39, 42–50	37, 40, 41
P75	Mechanical	1–11, 13–18, 20–23, 26 **42**	12, 19, 25 **18**	27–30, 32–45 **35**	24, 31
(42)	Reasoning	1–11, 13–17, 19, 20, 23, 28, 29, 33	12, 21, 30	26, 31, 34–50	18, 22, 24, 25, 27, 32
P50	Mechanical	1–4, 6–12, 14, 15, 17, 18, 20, 21 **32**	5, 13, 16, 19 **18**	24, 26–45 **45**	22, 23, 25
(32)	Reasoning	1–5, 8–11, 13, 14, 17, 20, 23	6, 12, 16, 19, 27, 28	21, 25, 26, 30–50	7, 15, 18, 22, 24, 29
P25	Mechanical	1–4, 6–9, 11, 12, 15 **21**	13, 16, 20 **21**	19, 22–45 **53**	5, 10, 14, 17, 18, 21
(21)	Reasoning	1–4, 8, 11, 17	6, 12, 16, 19, 22	15, 18, 21, 24–50	5, 7, 9, 10, 13, 14, 20, 23

level and 12 at the P90 level. At the P75, P50 and P20 levels there were 76, 100 and 58 scripts for pupils who had scored 42, 32 and 21 respectively and from each of these, 20 scripts were selected.

If one-half or more of the selected pupils at a given level were correct on their attempts at an item, this item was included in the column 'Items answered correctly' in table 4. The entries in the columns 'Items answered wrongly' and 'Items not attempted' were obtained in the same way. There were, however, some items in which there was no majority verdict; for example, eight of the twenty pupils were correct, six wrong, and six made no attempt in one item. It and similar items were placed in the column 'Items not classified'. The heading might equally well have been 'wrong or not attempted'; the point is that only a minority were correct.

This procedure overestimates the number of items answered correctly by the above average pupil and underestimates the score of the under average pupil. To avoid misunderstanding, the average numbers of correct responses, and of other types of response, have been printed in bold type in the appropriate sections of the table.

The general impression conveyed by these figures is that the higher scores were obtained by pupils who not only attempted more questions but also showed more accuracy in their responses.

One feature of the results is the large number of items in both sections of the test which were not attempted even by the above average pupils. In the mechanical arithmetic section the average number of items left unattempted ranged from 12 at the P95 level to 24 at the P25 level. In the arithmetical reasoning section the numbers ranged from 11 at the P95 level to 29 at the P25 level. It would seem that the test was too long and too difficult at this stage.

It must be borne in mind that the test had to be made sufficiently difficult to allow room for the very able pupils in the following year to show how much progress they had made. A similar analysis was therefore made of the performance of the pupils at the 90th and 95th percentiles in 1961. This showed that even the most able pupils in 1961 found the time allowance inadequate.

The first twelve items of the test in mechanical arithmetic were dealt with competently at almost all of the five levels of attainment studied. At item 12 the pupils at the P25 level had reached their limit, and the average pupils had reached theirs by item 21. This limit, as has been stated, may well have been imposed by lack of time rather than by the difficulty of the arithmetic.

Items involving decimal fractions (numbers 20–25, 27) were difficult for both the average and the less able pupils and even those at the P75 level were successful only with the simpler examples.

The average and above average pupils were highly successful with items involving the four basic rules and their application to money, length, weights and measures and vulgar fractions. The less able pupils had less success with vulgar fractions and weights and measures but, apart from an occasional error, showed a good knowledge of the four basic rules and their application to money and length.

In the arithmetical reasoning section of the paper only items 1 to 4, 8 and 11 were answered correctly at all levels, although 13 and 14 neared this standard. These involved money, speed, weights and time. Apparently straightforward calculation such as that of item 12 (*What is the area in square yards of a rectangular plot 36 feet long and 24 feet broad?*) were too difficult for all but the P95 and P90 pupils; this is all the more puzzling since item 14 (*A rectangular lawn measuring 5 yards by 6 yards is to be sown at a cost of 9d per square yard. What is the total cost?*) was well done. The less able pupils had almost reached their limit by item 4, though they also answered correctly items 8, 11 and 17. The average pupils reached item 14, with a few errors or omissions *en route*, and thereafter had only occasional successes. The abler pupils (P75) reached item 20 with occasional lapses and the best (P95) reached item 34 with only one lapse, at item 18.

The abler pupils answered correctly about three-quarters of the arithmetical items they attempted, whereas the average pupils answered correctly two-thirds and the less able pupils just under a half of the questions they attempted.

DISTRIBUTION OF TOTAL SCORES IN ENGLISH

The distribution of total scores on the English test is shown in figure 4. The scores of the 3492 pupils who were given the test have been grouped in class intervals of five. The table of frequencies on which the diagram is based is given in Appendix E, table 87.

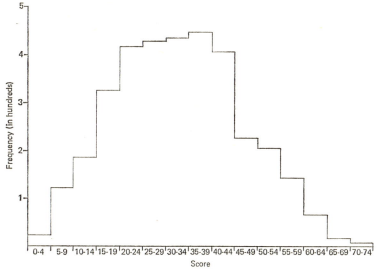

FIGURE 6   Distribution of total scores in English (1960)

MEDIANS AND QUARTILES FOR THE ENGLISH TEST

The maximum possible score on the test was 76. The average score on the test was 32·6. Table 5 gives the median and quartile scores for each section of the test and for the complete test. The percentile appropriate to each of the possible scores is given in Appendix E, table 89.

TABLE 5

QUARTILE AND MEDIAN SCORES FOR ENGLISH TEST

Section of test	Q1	Median	Q3	Maximum mark
1 Homonyms	3·3	4·5	5·3	6
2 Punctuation	1·7	3·3	5·1	10
3 Spelling	5·9	9·5	13·1	20
4 English usage	4·4	6·1	7·6	10
5 Vocabulary	2·1	3·9	6·1	10
6 Vocabulary (word building by definition)	2·6	5·0	7·8	20
Complete test	22·3	32·2	42·4	76

PERFORMANCE ON THE VARIOUS ITEMS OF THE ENGLISH TEST

The answer pattern for the items of the English test was obtained in the same way as for the arithmetic tests and is given in Appendix E, table 91. It is also shown diagrammatically in figure 7.

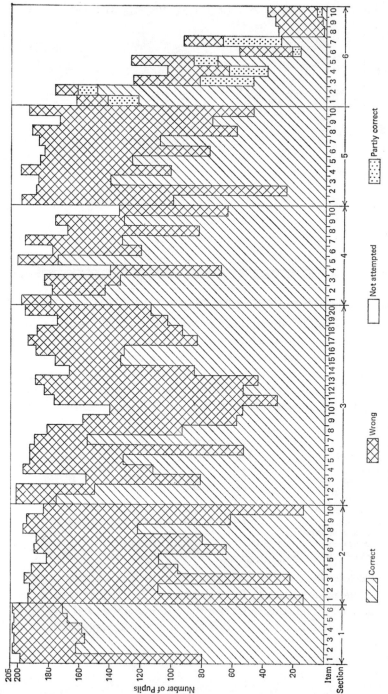

FIGURE 7   Answer pattern of test in English (1960 data)

PERFORMANCE OF TYPICAL PUPILS

The most representative response for each item of the English test at three pupil levels was calculated in the same way as that used for the arithmetic tests. Table 6 shows the results of this analysis.

TABLE 6

RESPONSES TO ITEMS OF ENGLISH TEST BY PUPILS AT DIFFERENT LEVELS OF TOTAL SCORE

Level	Section of test	Items answered correctly	Items answered wrongly	Items not attempted	Items not classified
Upper quartile (P75)	1 Homonyms	2–6	1		
	2 Punctuation	2, 4, 5, 7–9	1, 3, 6, 10		
	3 Spelling	1–9, 15–20	11–14		10
		42	**23**	**11**	
	4 English usage	1–3, 5–7, 9	8		4, 10
	5 Vocabulary	1, 3–7	2, 8–10		
	6 Word building	1a, 1b, 2a		3b, 3d–3f	2b, 3a, 3c
Median (P50)	1 Homonyms	2–6	1		
	2 Punctuation	2, 8	1, 3–7, 9, 10		
	3 Spelling	1, 2, 4, 5, 7, 15, 16, 19, 20	6, 10–14, 17, 18		3, 8, 9
		32	**30**	**14**	
	4 English usage	1–3, 5–7, 9	10		4, 8
	5 Vocabulary	3, 5	1, 2, 4, 6–10		
	6 Word building	1a, 1b, 2a		2b, 3b–3f	3a
Lower quartile (P25)	1 Homonyms	2–6	1		
	2 Punctuation		1–4, 6, 7, 9, 10		5, 8
	3 Spelling	1–2, 7, 15, 16	3–6, 8, 10–14, 17–20		9
		22	**36**	**18**	
	4 English usage	1–3, 5, 7	8		4, 6, 9, 10
	5 Vocabulary	5	1–4, 6–10		
	6 Word building	1a, 1b		2a, 2b, 3a–3f	

In this test the higher scores made by the typical above average pupils were obviously due largely to greater accuracy of response than to speed. The great majority of the items not attempted, at all levels of ability considered, were in the latter part of the last section of the test. This would suggest that the time allowance for the test was satisfactory.

Section 1 of the test dealt with homonyms and was answered well by all three groups, but item 1 *The coat is (hers, her's, hers')* was answered correctly only by a minority at all three levels.

Section 2 of the test dealt with punctuation. At the upper and average levels, pupils showed knowledge of the question mark (item 2) but only a minority at even the upper level supplied either a period or a semi-colon at the end of the first clause in item 1. Most of those at the lower quartile were unable to supply the apostrophe at *can't* (item 8) while those at the upper quartile were the only group to show familiarity with the use of commas, inverted commas and apostrophe in various forms (items 4–9). Only a small minority in any group used correctly the exclamation mark (item 3) and colon (item 10). All of the items in this section were too difficult for the under average pupil.

Section 3 consisted of completing and spelling words and, as one might expect, the abler pupils answered more accurately. Those at the upper quartile correctly spelt fifteen words, those at the median nine, and those at the lower quartile five. All three groups spelt correctly *Saturday, February, heard, exercise, succeed.* Only a minority in any group could spell *accommodation, practise, privilege, independent.*

Section 4 dealt with grammar and syntax, the questions involving the correction of sentences. On the whole, this section was answered equally well by all three groups, each group answering correctly at least five of the ten questions. However, items 4, 8 and 10 proved difficult at all levels. Item 4, *Do not waste your time like your brother does,* involved the correct use of *as* instead of *like*; item 8, *One may do as he likes in his own house,* required consistent use of the pronoun throughout the sentence; item 10, *The committee requests subscriptions to be paid to the treasurer,* involved dealing with confusion of constructions.

Section 5 dealt with the meanings of ten words. The questions were of the multiple choice type, where the pupil was required to choose his answer from five alternatives. Pupils at the upper quartile gave six of the ten meanings correctly, whereas those at the lower quartile were successful on one item only; this was

reluctant. The median group could add to this only *rectify.*
Only the upper group answered *oriental, credible, pensive* and
agility correctly. Only a minority in each group knew the
meanings of *chronic, assent, furtive* and *diligent.*

Section 6 consisted of ten questions in which the pupil was
required to construct a verb which had the same meaning as a
given phrase. In this section none of the groups attempted the
last three items, probably because of difficulty rather than lack
of time. Those at the lower quartile answered correctly the
only two questions which they attempted. Those at the median
scored on the same two items and on a third, had only partial
success on another, and did not attempt the remainder. Those
at the upper quartile attempted six items and scored on three
of them. All groups answered questions 1 (*a*) and 1 (*b*) correctly,
ie, (*a*) *simplify—to make easier* (*b*) *magnify—to make something
appear bigger*, although the spelling was not always accurate.
Only a minority in each group could provide *imitate, anticipate*
or *accelerate*, while only about one in a hundred gave *supplicate,
mitigate* or *alleviate.*

The test as a whole was a test of English language and usage.
The highest scorers showed their supremacy in superior
vocabulary, spelling, and punctuation, whereas the sections
dealing with English usage were answered reasonably well by
all pupils. The abler pupils answered correctly about two-
thirds of the questions they attempted, whereas the average
pupils answered correctly just over a half, and the less able
pupils just over a third.

DISTRIBUTION OF SCORES IN COMPOSITION

The title of the composition was 'What I think about jobs'.
The method of marking the composition is discussed fully in
Appendix A. Originally the compositions were marked on a
scale A, B, C, D, E and the scores of the 3456 pupils who were
given this test are given in table 7.

Almost 80 per cent were classified as either B, C, or D.
Specimen compositions corresponding to each of the gradings
A, B, C, D, E are given on pages 79 to 81 to show the standards
achieved.

TABLE 7

DISTRIBUTION OF COMPOSITION GRADES (1960)

Grade	Frequency	Percentage
A	288	8·3
B	644	18·6
C	1340	38·8
D	769	22·3
E	415	12·0
Total	3456	100·0

Some markers made use of a refinement by which categories C+ and C− were also used. The scale was then transformed to the numerical scale shown below, in which the categories C+ and C− are given separate numbers from the basic ratings.

Grading	A	B	C+	C	C−	D	E	None	Unknown
Score	8	7	6	5	4	3	2	0	X

When no composition sheet was available the entry was the usual X. There were, however, a few cases in which the pupil had entered the appropriate particulars at the head of the sheet but had written no composition. These were coded as O. The distributions of scores by sex and type of course are given in Appendix E, table 88.

SUMMARY OF CHAPTER

In this chapter an effort has been made to depict the performance of the group of 15-year-olds in the tests of arithmetic, English, and composition. It is hoped that the data provide a picture of the attainments of these young people of 1960 in the basic skills.

The above average pupils could successfully apply their knowledge of the basic arithmetical processes to money, length, weights and measures. They had a good knowledge of vulgar fractions, but were able to tackle only the simpler problems in decimal notation (probably through lack of time). In English, they showed a good knowledge of punctuation. They were also able to spell correctly at least fifteen words out of twenty, but they had difficulty with words like *accommodation*, *privilege* and *independent*. Their knowledge of English usage was good. In vocabulary they knew the meaning of words such as *credible* and *pensive*, but did not know the meaning of *chronic* or *assent*. In all they were able to answer correctly three-quarters or more of the arithmetic items and two-thirds or more of the English items they attempted.

The average pupils could apply their knowledge of the basic arithmetical processes to money, length, weights and measures. They also had a good knowledge of vulgar fractions but were unsure in their handling of decimal fractions. In English they made low scores in punctuation, and could spell only ten of the twenty words in the test, being defeated by words like *disappointed* and *inconvenient*. Their knowledge of English usage was fairly good. In vocabulary they knew the meanings of *rectify* and *reluctant* but were uncertain about *pensive* and more difficult words in the list. In all, they were able to answer correctly about two-thirds of the arithmetic and half of the English items which they attempted.

The under average pupils had a good knowledge of the four basic arithmetic rules and could apply them to money and length. They had less success with weights and measures and with vulgar fractions. In English they found the test of punctuation to be difficult and they could spell only five of the twenty words in the test. Their knowledge of English usage was fairly good. In vocabulary they knew the meaning of *reluctant* but were unfamiliar with the other words. In all, they were able to answer half of the arithmetic and one-third of the English items they attempted.

The picture would be incomplete without a reference to the extremes—the two or three pupils who completed correctly practically the whole of the test, or the few who could not make even a handful of correct responses in either arithmetic or English. The numbers are small but they demonstrate once again the range of attainments to be found in any age-group.

TYPICAL COMPOSITIONS
What I think about jobs

Grade A

My opinion of jobs is that if they were not necessary for survival there would be many people unemployed. Our race is naturally lazy and man only works for the essentials to exist. Many people who cannot supposedly get jobs have to depend on National Assistance but I think if one is desperate one can get some sort of job, however bad.   If someone really to improve their status in life it is only willpower, determination and hard work that will help them to succeed.

Personally, I do not wish to attempt my 'Highers' as I think there are many excellent jobs, in my line of work, in which no 'Highers' are necessary.

One hears of many strikes nowadays which are caused by numerous grievances the workers have.   These strikes are caused by ignorant people and an employer does not know what to expect of them.   The strikers do not think of the hardships their families have to suffer when there is only one wage to depend on.

Grade B

When you start work, you are better to have a job waiting for you.   A job with a small pay, is all very well, if you get so much rises a year, but if the small pay does not increase yearly it would be better to find a well paying job.

If you go in for a trade, such as printing, you do not start with a big wage but you get a rise every six months. When you have finished your time the wage stays the same all the rest of the time.   I myself wish to sit the exams for the Civil Service. The wage in the Civil Service high but the work is hard.   If you go into the Civil Service for typing alone, you never stop typing from morn till night but with shorthand and typing you get a break from typing to take down some shorthand.   The speeds you have to be able to do in the exams are 100 wpm in shorthand and 40 wpm in typing.

Working with animals is not a good paying job but it is always interesting.   If you work with animals, it is better not to be too friendly with one certain animal, because if it dies, you may be broken hearted.

A scientist's secretary is also very well paying and very interesting indeed, with all the different experiments. You need to be very well experienced to be a scientist's secretary.

Grade C

I think that jobs in Scotland are very hard to come by especially for people just left school, and even if they are lucky enough to get one they do not start on it right away.   They do things like making tea and running errands for the higher up employees.

At Prestwick airport for instance they are always paying off hundreds of men because they are not getting enough orders for building planes.

Shop jobs are quite easy to come by but they don't have much future.   I think that the best kind of jobs to get are jobs at hospitals nursing, cooks and orderlys and at offices or as cashiers, and as telephonist a girl has a good job.   But there is still not enough jobs for everybody.

Grade D

What I think about Jobs, I think some jobs are good other I don't the kind of job I would like to work in is a shop a shop that sells baby clothe and one or to thing for growing up children.   The job I would not like to work in is a factory in most factory you have just to put any old thing on to go out in.   When you work in a shop or be a hairdresser you can go with your best thing on because you are not going to go and get them dirty of a machine I would like to work in a shop that opens about 9 o clock as I think that is a reonable time.

Grade E

I think a good health job is good for a persons health.   Out in the country away from big towns you get freesh health air instead of smog from chimenes pots.

On a farm you get hundreds of good jobs and when it is raining you work inside, except in several ocasions.   During the summer you get all the sun that is about and the nice smell of the harvast.   I will be clad to start that kind of life when I leave the school.

Getting up early is good for you so that is a good way of doing it so I preefer farm life better than enithing eles.

6

Chapter 6

A FURTHER ANALYSIS OF SCORES AT 15

INTRODUCTION

The preceding chapter has given a picture of the scores made by the whole group in the tests of arithmetic, English, and composition. The group was composed of boys and girls from different areas, following different types of course, some intending to leave school in a few months, others intending to continue for a further year or more, living in different sizes of house, having fathers with very different occupations, and looking forward to different occupations when they themselves were grown-up. It would therefore seem worthwhile to examine the scores made by the pupils in the various sub-groups into which the total groups can be divided and to estimate the degree of relationship between the scores and these different circumstances.

We shall take them in order of malleability, beginning with those that cannot readily be changed (sex of pupil, father's occupation), continuing with those which are more malleable (authority area—in that an authority might change its policy, size of house), and finishing with those that are most malleable (type of school course, reason for leaving school, and job preferred when grown-up). The last two might be regarded as end-products of the same type as the attainments in the tests themselves.

COMPARISON OF ACHIEVEMENTS OF BOYS AND GIRLS

Table 8 gives the mean scores of the 1836 boys and 1711 girls in the group for each test and for each section of each test. The frequency distributions of the main test scores for boys and girls are given in Appendix E, tables 86, 87, 88.

It will be observed that the girls were slightly superior to the boys in mechanical arithmetic but were slightly inferior on the arithmetical reasoning section.   There was no difference on overall arithmetic scores.   In English the girls were superior in most sub-tests and in total scores; in composition they were again superior.

TABLE 8

MEAN SCORES ON TESTS AND SUB-TESTS ANALYSED BY SEX

| | Mean score | |
Test	Boys	Girls
Mechanical arithmetic	16·3	17·2
Arithmetical reasoning	16·1	15·1
Arithmetic test—overall	32·4 (P50)[1]	32·4 (P50)
English homonyms	4·0	4·5
English punctuation	3·2	3·8
English spelling	8·4	10·6
English usage	5·5	6·3
English vocabulary	4·1	4·2
English word building	5·3	5·3
English test—overall	30·6 (P46)	34·8 (P56)
Composition	4·5	5·2

The question arises whether the differences found can be regarded as statistically significant.   In the present context this question is whether they would have arisen if 1836 pupils had been selected at random, irrespective of sex, and their average score compared with that of the remaining 1711 pupils.   The answer to that question is that differences as large as 0·9 or 1·0 in either of the arithmetic tests would have arisen less than once in a hundred samples of that kind; they are therefore regarded as statistically significant.   Whether they are educationally significant is another question.   They correspond to differences between the 48th and the 52nd places on the percentile scale and are therefore not of much educational significance.

In English, on the other hand, the superiority of the girls represents the difference between the 56th place and 46th place on a percentile scale and is more substantial, as well as being statistically significant.   This superiority was shown in the first four sections of the test, but not in the sections dealing with work building and vocabulary.

In the composition test the girls again proved superior to the boys.

[1] For definition of P50, see p 66.

The system used to classify father's occupation was one pre-viously used by the Council in its Mental Surveys. It was not intended to be a hierarchical classification.

Class	Father's occupation
1	Professionally qualified or employing large staff
2	Self-employed, or employing small staff
3	Salaried employees not professionally qualified
4	Non-manual wage earners
5	Skilled manual wage earners
6	Semi-skilled manual wage earners
7	Unskilled manual wage earners
8	Farmers
9	Agricultural workers
Y	Unemployed
O	Father dead or other person named as guardian
X	Unknown

Table 9 gives a summary of the mean scores and percentiles for each occupational class.

TABLE 9

RELATION OF MEAN SCORES AND CORRESPONDING PERCENTILES TO FATHER'S OCCUPATION

Father's occupational class	Arithmetic		English		Composition	
	Score	Percentile	Score	Percentile	Score	No in category
1	46·6	82	46·7	84	6·6	139
2	37·6	64	37·9	64	5·6	113
3	36·7	62	39·5	68	5·5	151
4	35·3	59	36·0	59	5·2	361
5	33·6	54	34·3	55	5·1	812
6	30·4	46	30·2	45	4·5	935
7	27·3	39	27·3	37	4·2	361
8	33·5	54	32·5	51	4·6	75
9	29·6	44	29·6	43	4·6	139
Y	26·6	37	25·6	34	3·9	55
O	31·1	47	30·5	46	4·6	271
Unknown	27·4	39	27·1	37	4·2	135
					Total	3547

When more than two means are being compared, the appropri-ate statistical technique is analysis of variance. The hypothesis to be tested is that the differences found between means would have arisen if the various sub-groups had been chosen at random from the total group. The analyses[1] showed that many of the differences were too large to be accounted for in this way; the achievements of the pupils were related to the occupational class of their fathers. If classes 8 (farmers), 9 (agricultural workers), O (guardian names) are excluded, the order of occupational classes conformed closely to that of the order of magnitude of the mean scores in each of the three subjects tested.

These findings agree very closely with those of the Scottish Mental Survey of 1947, in which the pupils were aged 11 and the test was a group test of intelligence. The relationship is discussed in some detail in one of the reports of the Survey[2] and the discussion will not be repeated here. But it is necessary to stress, as is done in the Mental Survey report, the wide range of scores for any occupation and of occupations for any score. This is done in tables 10 and 11, in which high scorers are those in the top 20 per cent (approximately) of the distribution; average to high are those between P80 and P50; low to average are those between P50 and P20, and low scorers are those in the bottom 20 per cent (approximately).

TABLE 10

RELATION BETWEEN ATTAINMENT IN ARITHMETIC AND
FATHER'S OCCUPATION

Numbers of pupils

					Father's occupation								
Level of score	*1*	*2*	*3*	*4*	*5*	*6*	*7*	*8*	*9*	*Y*	*O*	*X*	*Total*
High	69	34	41	99	176	158	43	16	24	9	49	20	738
Average to high	46	33	51	96	244	235	80	21	34	9	72	25	946
Low to average	20	26	39	103	248	298	117	23	40	15	76	34	1039
Low	1	16	16	53	132	225	115	12	40	20	62	50	742
Unknown	3	4	4	10	12	19	6	3	1	2	12	6	82
Totals	139	113	151	361	812	935	361	75	139	55	271	135	3547

It will be observed that almost half of the high scorers had fathers who belonged to the skilled and semi-skilled occupations compared with only 18 per cent whose fathers were professional or self-employed. Yet 38 per cent of pupils from the professional

[1] The method used to test the significance of the difference in each pair of means is that devised by Scheffé, and described in W L Hays' *Statistics for Psychologists*. New York: Holt, Rinehart and Winston, 1965.
[2] *Social Implications of the 1947 Scottish Mental Survey*, pp 43-50, Publication of the Scottish Council for Research in Education, 35. London: University of London Press Ltd, 1953.

and self-employed group were high scorers compared with only 20 per cent of pupils from the skilled and semi-skilled group. The large weight of numbers in the skilled and semi-skilled groups more than compensates for the smaller chance of being above average.

TABLE 11

RELATION BETWEEN ATTAINMENT IN ENGLISH AND FATHER'S OCCUPATION

Numbers of pupils

					Father's occupation								
Level of score	1	2	3	4	5	6	7	8	9	Y	O	X	Total
High	79	42	58	105	176	119	32	14	20	4	43	15	707
Average to high	44	32	50	107	269	275	82	24	36	10	72	29	1030
Low to average	13	25	28	103	247	322	139	24	45	23	83	48	1100
Low	1	13	15	44	108	197	103	12	38	18	66	40	655
Unknown	2	1	0	2	12	22	5	1	0	0	7	3	55
Totals	139	113	151	361	812	935	361	75	139	55	271	135	3547

Interesting examples of variations from the general pattern include the girl who scored 89 (P100) in arithmetic and 56 (P96) in English, whose father was a shipyard plater's help (category 6); the boy who scored 82 (P100) in arithmetic and 56 (P96) in English, whose father was a roadworks labourer (category 7); and the girl who scored 76 (P100) in arithmetic and 63 (P99) in English, whose father was a gardener (category 9). On the other hand, no pupil whose father was professionally qualified or an employer of a large staff scored less than 17 (P18) in arithmetic or 17 (P14) in English.

COMPARISON OF ACHIEVEMENTS OF PUPILS
IN DIFFERENT AREAS

In chapter 2 it was stated that the pupils tested were drawn from five areas in Scotland, four of the five being administered by separate education authorities and the fifth being the industrial part of still another education authority area.

The mean scores obtained by the pupils in the five areas are shown in table 12. The distributions of scores are shown in Appendix E, tables 86 and 87.

Analysis of variance showed that the differences among the means were too large to be attributed to sampling variations. The data do not suggest any simple cause for these differences.

TABLE 12

MEAN SCORES AND PERCENTILES OBTAINED IN THE FIVE AREAS

Area

	1	2	3	4	5	Total
Arithmetic	33·1 (P53)	28·9 (P42)	32·1 (P50)	33·2 (P53)	30·4 (P46)	32·4
English	32·7 (P51)	31·3 (P47)	32·6 (P51)	32·1 (P50)	35·2 (P57)	32·6

RELATION OF TEST SCORES TO RATEABLE VALUE OF HOUSE

As mentioned previously in chapter 4, the Committee decided to use the rateable value of the house in which the young person lived as a measure of the socio-economic status of each pupil. The rateable value of each house was obtained from the appropriate valuation roll. Table 13 gives a summary of the mean scores and corresponding percentiles for each level of rateable value.

TABLE 13

MEAN SCORES AND PERCENTILES ON TESTS FOR DIFFERENT
LEVELS OF RATEABLE VALUE OF HOUSE OCCUPIED

Rateable value of house in £	Arithmetic		English		Composition	No in
	Score	Percentile	Score	Percentile	Score	category
60–99	41·3	73	41·6	73	5·8	158
50–59	35·2	58	35·8	59	5·1	298
40–49	32·3	51	32·7	51	5·0	640
34–39	30·9	47	31·6	48	4·7	754
30–33	31·5	49	31·3	47	4·5	646
20–29	32·9	52	33·0	52	4·8	555
0–19	31·0	47	29·7	43	4·6	349
Unknown	29·7	44	32·0	49	4·7	147
					Total	3547

When the differences among the means were examined in the usual way, the analysis showed that some of the differences were too large to be accounted for as sampling fluctuations. In arithmetic, English and composition, the pupils in houses rated £60 and over made significantly higher scores than did the others. For houses rated under £50 there were no statistically significant differences in score among the five sets of rateable values.

Within any one category there were considerable variations in achievement. Worthy of mention is the girl who scored 89 (P100), the highest mark in the 1960 arithmetic test. She lived in a house with a rateable value of £13. Another girl who scored 67 (P100) in English lived in a house with a rateable value of £16. A boy who lived in a house with a rateable value of £38 scored 85 (P100) in arithmetic and 67 (P100) in English. On the other hand, a boy living in a house rated at £77 could score only 9 (P6) in arithmetic and 10 (P5) in English, while another living in a house rated at £67 could score only 4 (P1) in arithmetic and 6 (P1) in English.

In general, however, children from the most highly rated houses scored higher marks than children from houses of moderate or low rateable value. While this is true, one must

TABLE 14

RELATION OF ARITHMETIC SCORE TO SOCIO-ECONOMIC LEVEL

	Numbers of pupils in houses with rateable value				
Scores	Low	Medium	High	Unknown	Total
High	188	369	155	26	738
Medium	489	1203	213	80	1985
Low	203	423	77	39	742
Unknown	24	45	11	2	82
Totals	904	2040	456	147	3547

bear in mind the large numbers of the above average pupils who come from homes of medium and lower socio-economic level. The majority of high scorers indeed do not come from homes of high rateable value as table 14 indicates. There were, in fact, more high scorers from the houses with low rateable value.

Table 14 was obtained by summation from the frequency distribution of arithmetic scores. High scores are those above the 80th percentile level, low scores are those below the 20th percentile level. High rateable value was taken as £50 and above; low rateable value was taken as below £30. A similar picture was found for the results of the English test and has therefore not been included here.

The figures in table 14 emphasise once again that a positive association between two variables may leave room for a considerable range in one for a given value of the other. Although 35 per cent of the pupils from high-rated houses were high scorers, compared with only 19 per cent from other houses, the greatest number of high scorers came from the less highly rated houses. In fact there was a greater number of high scorers from the houses with rateable value below £30 than there was from houses rated at £50 and above. The apparent contradiction arises from the low proportion of highly rated houses in the group as a whole.

COMPARISON OF ACHIEVEMENTS OF PUPILS IN
SENIOR SECONDARY AND JUNIOR SECONDARY COURSES

Pupils were classified as senior secondary pupils if they were following a course leading to the Scottish Leaving Certificate (as it was then named); otherwise they were classified as junior secondary pupils. The frequency distributions of test scores for the two types of courses are given in Appendix E, tables 86, 87, 88.

Table 15 gives the mean scores of both groups of pupils for each test and for each section of each test.

TABLE 15

MEAN SCORES ON TESTS FOR DIFFERENT TYPES OF COURSE

Test	Senior secondary	Junior secondary
Mechanical arithmetic	21·9	14·4
Arithmetical reasoning	23·5	12·1
Arithmetic test—overall	45·4 (P81)	26·5 (P37)
English homonyms	5·1	3·9
English punctuation	5·5	2·6
English spelling	13·1	7·8
English usage	7·6	5·2
English vocabulary	6·4	3·2
English word building	7·9	4·1
English test—overall	45·6 (P82)	26·7 (P36)
Composition	6·2	4·2

In each case the senior secondary pupils had a higher mean score than the junior secondary pupils and the differences are large. The average senior secondary pupil scored at the 80th percentile level (calculated from the total population) in both English and arithmetic, whereas the average junior secondary pupil scored at the 35th percentile level. There is no doubt about the statistical significance of these differences. Nevertheless, there was a considerable amount of overlap between the two groups, some senior secondary pupils scoring as low as the 6th percentile in arithmetic and the 14th percentile in English, while some junior secondary pupils scored as high as the 99th percentile in the English and arithmetic tests. One junior secondary pupil scored 82 (P100) in the 1960 arithmetic test, a score achieved or bettered by only six senior secondary pupils.

REASON FOR LEAVING SCHOOL

The reasons given for pupils leaving school have been studied in earlier researches, but in most cases the pupils concerned have been those in grammar school types of course. The Crowther Report[1] said

> The great majority of those who left school as soon as the law permitted had attended modern or all-age schools and we know that in the early 1950s such schools had generally little, if any, provision for continued education beyond 15. In these cases it seemed profitless to search for reasons for early school-leaving other than that to leave was customary and, often, almost inevitable. Ninety per cent of the 15-year-old leavers fell into this category. The concern of this enquiry therefore lay with the other 10 per cent.

The report on early leaving[2] was also concerned with those leaving secondary schools which provide courses beyond the minimum school-leaving age. Both of these reports were primarily concerned with the educational system of England and Wales.

The Scottish inquiry described in this volume dealt with practically the whole range of secondary education in Scotland (the only exclusion being that for mentally handicapped pupils). Following the technique of the *Early Leaving* inquiry, reasons for the pupil leaving were obtained both from the pupil and from his or her headmaster, so that the situation was seen from both the youthful and the adult angle.

After an examination of the main categories of reason for leaving given in *Early Leaving* (pp 69, 72, 94) and in *15 to 18* (Vol II, p 135), the sociological schedules completed by the headmaster or other member of staff and the short question-

---

[1] *15 to 18*, The Central Advisory Council for Education (England), Vol II, p 134. HMSO, 1960.
[2] *Early Leaving*, The Central Advisory Council for Education (England). HMSO, 1954.

naires completed by the pupils were inspected. It was found that most of the reasons given by the headmasters came under one or other of the categories used in the English reports, but some minor changes were made to suit the Scottish data.

RELATION OF TEST SCORES TO HEADMASTER'S REASON
FOR PUPIL LEAVING SCHOOL

The reason given by the headmaster for the pupil's leaving school was coded according to the following scheme.

Code No	Reason
0	Not leaving
1	Unwilling but forced to leave
2	Wishes to transfer to full-time further education
3	Finds school work difficult
4	Age, end of course
5	Prefers work to school
6	No interest in school work
7	Required at home
8	Money required
X	Not known or unclassified

Table 16 gives a summary of the mean scores for each classification.

TABLE 16

MEAN SCORES AND PERCENTILES CLASSIFIED BY HEADMASTER'S
REASON FOR PUPIL LEAVING SCHOOL

| Reason | Arithmetic | | English | | Composition | No of |
	Score	Percentile	Score	Percentile	Score	Pupils
0	45·1	80	45·8	82	6·3	929
1	39·2	68	35·6	58	4·8	18
2	35·0	58	34·7	56	5·1	127
3	35·4	59	38·1	64	5·5	28
4	26·2	36	26·5	36	4·1	1636
5	29·6	44	29·0	42	4·5	508
6	33·7	54	32·4	50	4·7	39
7	25·3	34	29·8	44	4·2	9
8	31·0	47	31·2	47	4·5	78
Unknown	27·0	38	27·2	37	4·5	175
					Total	3547

It is noteworthy that for 62 per cent of those who left school the reason given for leaving by the headmaster was age or end of course. This is in marked contrast to the reasons for leaving given by the pupils (cf table 17). A further 19 per cent of the group were said to be leaving because they preferred work to school.

Category 0 comprised those pupils who were expected to remain at school. The superiority of this category relative to the others who were expected to leave school for one reason or another is very evident. Category 3 comprised those who, in the headmaster's opinion, were leaving because they found school work difficult and it is of interest that they appear to be pupils above average in achievement. This point is given further consideration in the next section, as also is the high frequency of responses in category 4.

RELATION OF TEST SCORES TO PUPIL'S REASON FOR
LEAVING SCHOOL

Each pupil entered in the composition paper his or her reason for leaving school and the responses were coded according to the scheme below.

Code No	Reason
0	Not leaving
1	Unwilling but forced to leave
2	Wish to transfer to full-time further education
3	Finds school work difficult
4	Age, end of course
5	Fear of unemployment
6	Wish to repay parents
7	Wish to see world, be in open air
8	Prefers work to school
9	Ten years enough, learned enough
X	No reason, or incomprehensible, or unclassified
Y	Doesn't like school, or teachers, or subject

This classification, like that for the headmasters, was based on a preliminary scrutiny of the responses given by the pupils to the open-ended question. It will be observed that there is a difference of opinion between headmaster and pupil as to the number returning to school (cf tables 16 and 17). Table 17 gives a summary of the mean score for each category.

Those pupils in category 3 who were leaving because they found school work difficult were of above average achievement and this result confirms the findings of the previous section. Of the 59, no fewer than 40 were in senior secondary courses. Most of them, and most of the 19 who were in junior secondary courses, made it fairly clear in their replies that they had in mind courses leading to presentation for the Higher grade in the Leaving Certificate examinations when they described the work as being difficult. This explains the apparent anomaly of abler pupils finding school work difficult.

TABLE 17

MEAN SCORES AND PERCENTILES CLASSIFIED BY PUPIL'S
REASON FOR LEAVING SCHOOL

| Reason | Arithmetic | | English | | Composition | No of |
	Score	Percentile	Score	Percentile	Score	Pupils
0	44·0	78	44·1	79	6·2	1008
1	35·9	60	33·0	52	4·6	30
2	33·3	53	35·5	58	5·1	92
3	36·2	61	36·2	60	5·1	59
4	27·0	38	27·6	38	4·2	250
5	27·5	39	26·1	35	4·3	51
6	26·1	36	25·9	34	4·1	213
7	26·3	36	27·0	37	4·1	119
8	27·3	38	27·4	37	4·2	1349
9	30·4	46	28·8	41	4·3	75
X	26·3	36	28·3	40	3·9	163
Y	27·4	39	27·2	37	4·1	138
					Total	3547

The pupils who were staying on at school (category 0) were obviously superior in their achievements to all the other categories. Excluding categories 1, 2, 3, where at least some interest in education was expressed by the pupil, there would appear to be little relationship between the pupil's reason for leaving school and his achievements in the basic subjects.

The differences between the reasons for leaving school given by headmasters and those given by their pupils are worthy of comment. The two major reasons given by the headmasters were 'age or end of course' (62 per cent) and 'prefers work to school' (19 per cent). The same two reasons were also the major ones quoted by their pupils but the proportions choosing them were quite different. 'Age' or 'end of course' was given by only 10 per cent of the pupils leaving school, whereas 'prefers work to school' was given by 53 per cent of them. It is rather disturbing to learn that it is the teachers rather than the pupils who accept that pupils of 15 are leaving school because that is the appropriate age to do so, or because they have completed their courses and school has apparently nothing more to offer them. The very term 'school-leaving age' seems to suggest that 15 is the correct age to leave; 'the end of compulsory schooling' or a similar phrase would be a better term.

The large percentage of pupils (53 per cent) who indicated that they 'prefer work to school' would appear to suggest that the schools are unable to preserve the interest of many of their pupils. This is borne out by some of the replies: 'a happy release', 'learent enuve', 'I am leaving because it is time up and 10 years at school is quiet a while', 'Because a have be at school to long and want to get out of it', 'I think my brain is full'. The recommendations of the Brunton Report[1] on the provision of vocationally-biassed courses may provide a possible remedy.

A substantial number wished to enlarge their horizons—'to see the world', 'to emigrate', 'I want an open-air life'—and an even larger number wished to repay their parents. Only 30 appeared to be leaving against their wishes. The category 'fear of unemployment' covers a relatively small group who feared that, as the year drew nearer in which the post-war 'bulge' would begin to leave school, continuing at school for a further year would prejudice rather than enhance their prospects of obtaining employment in their area.

RELATION BETWEEN TEST SCORES AND JOB PREFERRED
WHEN GROWN UP

In the short questionnaire which preceded the composition test the pupil was asked to state briefly what kind of job he or she would like to have when grown-up. A preliminary inspection of the replies showed that only a few were of the fantasy type; some were vague, but relatively few were uncertain or stated that they did not know. The responses were classified according to the scheme on facing page.

Table 18 gives a summary of the mean scores for each category.

The figures reveal an almost perfect correspondence between the hierarchical structure of 'job preferred' and achievement as

[1] *From School to Further Education.* HMSO, 1963.

measured by the tests and indicates a very strong association between the two. It would appear that pupils at the age of 15 are well aware of their proficiencies and deficiencies when looking forward to the kind of job that will suit them when they are grown-up.

Code No	Job
9	Major professional
8	Minor professional
7	Higher non-manual
6	Other non-manual
5	Skilled manual
4	Semi-skilled manual or shop
3	Factory
2	Unskilled manual, agriculture, domestic
X	Not known

This topic may be viewed from another aspect. What are the jobs preferred at the various levels of competence of the pupils? The figures are shown in tables 19 and 20, in which high scorers are defined as those above the 80th percentile,

TABLE 18

MEAN SCORES ON TESTS AND PERCENTILES FOR DIFFERENT CATEGORIES OF JOB PREFERRED WHEN GROWN UP

Job Preferred	Arithmetic		English		Composition	No in
	Score	Percentile	Score	Percentile	Score	Category
9	48·0	84	49·2	88	6·6	353
8	40·2	70	41·1	72	5·9	274
7	38·9	67	39·5	68	5·8	391
6	34·7	57	34·0	54	5·1	341
5	28·3	41	27·9	39	4·2	1203
4	24·5	32	24·6	31	3·8	541
3	21·5	26	23·3	28	3·8	128
2	21·9	27	21·7	24	3·2	33
X	31·3	48	33·3	52	5·0	283
					Total	3547

average to high are those between the 50th and 80th percentiles, low to average are those between the 20th and 50th percentiles and low are those below the 20th percentile. The highest frequency in each row has been shown in bold type.

The tables show the tendency for the high scorers to prefer the professions, and higher non-manual jobs, although there is a substantial proportion hoping to enter skilled manual work;

this type of work attracts young people from all levels of attainment. On the other hand, semi-skilled or unskilled manual occupations or that of shop assistant seem likely to be staffed by below average scorers. The mean scores of the prospective

TABLE 19

JOB PREFERENCES OF PUPILS AT FOUR LEVELS OF ARITHMETIC SCORE

| | | | | | | | | | Number of pupils | |
| | | | | | Type of job preferred | | | | | |
Level of Score	9	8	7	6	5	4	3	2	X	Total
High	203	105	120	69	140	41	2	1	57	738
Average to high	104	91	151	110	312	88	14	7	69	946
Low to average	34	52	98	134	377	196	58	11	79	1039
Low	6	23	16	23	344	195	52	14	69	742
Absent from test	6	3	6	5	30	21	2	0	9	82
Totals	353	274	391	341	1203	541	128	33	283	3547

shop assistants were 27·6 (P38) in arithmetic and 28·8 (P40) in English, but the range of scores covered practically the whole scale.

The exceptions to the general trends were, as usual, of some interest. One boy who scored 82 (P100) in arithmetic and 56

TABLE 20

JOB PREFERENCES OF PUPILS AT FOUR LEVELS OF ENGLISH SCORE

| | | | | | | | | | Number of pupils | |
| | | | | | Type of job preferred | | | | | |
Level of Score	9	8	7	6	5	4	3	2	X	Total
High	251	116	117	50	78	31	2	1	61	707
Average to high	81	98	179	141	334	105	23	5	64	1030
Low to average	17	42	80	119	496	206	52	15	73	1100
Low	4	17	13	28	289	194	51	11	48	655
Absent from test		1	2	3	6	5		1	37	55
Totals	353	274	391	341	1203	541	128	33	283	3547

(P96) in English looked forward to becoming a skilled engineer (category 5) at the age of 21. On the other hand, a boy who scored 2 (P0) in arithmetic and 1 (P0) in English and wished a major professional post, wrote 'I wood lick to be a capton'. Another boy who scored 6 (P1) in arithmetic and 9 (P3) in English wished to be a chief engineer on a tanker when he grew up while a third who scored 13 (P7) in English and did not sit the arithmetic test wished to be a veterinary surgeon.

SUMMARY OF CHAPTER

This chapter has shown the differences in the scores achieved by various sub-groups of the population tested in 1960. While the relatively large numbers have enabled statistical significance to be established for many of the differences, the main impression is one of considerable overlap of scores in the various sub-groups. To say that the girls were superior to the boys in the English test does not mean that every girl made a higher score than every boy, but only that the average performance was higher. This caution must be borne in mind in reading the following summary.

Girls were slightly superior to boys in mechanical arithmetic and slightly inferior in arithmetical reasoning. As has been stated, they were superior in the English test and also in composition. The differences in average score among the authority areas were slight. There was a marked association between score and socio-economic status as measured by father's occupation, and a similar association, though not so strongly marked, between score and rateable value of house.

As one would expect, the pupils in senior secondary courses had higher achievements, on average, than those in junior secondary courses. Those who intended to return to school had higher achievements than those intending to leave at the earliest opportunity, but otherwise there was no association between score and reason for leaving. It is probably worthy of note in this summary that the commonest reason given by *pupils* for leaving school was 'prefers work to school', while the majority of the *teachers* gave 'age' or 'end of course' as the reason.

The 'job preferred' by the pupils was found to be strongly associated with achievement. The young people appeared to be well aware of their abilities and to have chosen their future employment accordingly. There was a marked difference in level of attainment between those who wished to take up non-manual or professional occupations and those selecting factory or unskilled employment. But the 'skilled manual' category drew its prospective employees from all levels of attainment.

7

While it is true that pupils from homes with parents in professional or non-manual occupations were more likely than other pupils to have high scores, the bulk of the high scoring pupils were in fact drawn from the homes of the skilled and semi-skilled manual workers. The same may also be said of the average and of the low scoring pupils; it is a consequence of the high proportion of the population included in these occupational categories.

The main correlates of score in the tests were, then, type of secondary courses followed and job preferred when grown up. A survey such as that reported here can give little or no guidance on causal relationships. It is at least a plausible hypothesis that all three correlates are outcomes of other variables—for example, the ability and attainment of the pupil on entry to the secondary course—of which we have no measure in the present investigation.

Chapter 7

WHAT THEY DID BETWEEN 15 AND 16

INTRODUCTION

As has been indicated in chapter 3, only 1798, or 51 per cent of the 1960 group, could be persuaded to take the tests and answer the questionnaires in 1961. The information which we have about their careers in 1960–61 is therefore derived from

TABLE 21

DISTRIBUTIONS OF SCORES IN ARITHMETIC, ENGLISH AND COMPOSITION FOR THE 1960 AND 1961 GROUPS

	Arithmetic			English				Composition		
	Numbers tested		Percent-age	Numbers tested		Percent-age		Numbers tested		Percent-age
1960 score	1960	1961	re-tested	1960	1961	re-tested	1960 score	1960	1961	re-tested
80–89	7	5	71							
70–79	36	32	89	3	3	100	8	288	232	81
60–69	111	89	80	81	68	84	7	644	425	66
50–59	320	261	82	346	281	81	6	191	97	51
40–49	618	398	64	683	443	65	5	940	492	52
30–39	857	451	53	880	444	51	4	209	85	41
20–29	774	314	41	844	328	39	3	769	303	39
10–19	502	155	31	512	171	33	2	408	121	30
0–9	240	54	23	143	29	20	0	7	2	29
Absent	82	39	48	55	31	56		91	41	45
Total	3547	1798	51	3547	1798	51		3547	1798	51

only half of the original group. Nor can the half who did turn out be taken to be a representative sample of the whole group, as a glance at table 21 will show. In this table, those recorded as absent for one test had appeared for another or had completed the questionnaire.

This table gives a clear indication that the group re-tested in 1961 cannot be regarded as representative of the 1960 group in any of the three subject areas. The proportions attending for the 1961 tests are relatively high for the high scorers of 1960 and fall away at a fairly steady rate as the 1960 score levels fall, until at the lowest level of 1960 score only about 20 to 25 per

cent are available. In the ensuing discussions we must therefore bear in mind that the information has been obtained from
a biassed sample in which the lower scorers are less and less
adequately represented as the scores decrease.

From the information available in the questionnaires which
were completed in March 1961 it was possible to ascertain what
the young people who were re-tested had been doing in the ten
months subsequent to the first testing. The type of job actually
taken up by the young people, their leisure activities, the books
and newspapers they read could all be investigated. The
details of this investigation are given in this chapter.

OCCUPATION IN 1960–61 AND ITS RELATION TO 1960 SCORES

The occupations actually taken up by the re-test group were
coded as follows.

Code No	Type of occupation	No in category
8	Professional	4
7	Higher non-manual (boys) Skilled clerical (girls)	26
6	Lower non-manual (boys) Other clerical (girls)	227
5	Skilled manual	277
4	Semi-skilled manual (boys) Shop (girls)	258
3	Factory	94
2	Unskilled manual, agriculture (boys) Domestic (girls)	50
1	Full-time further education	160
0	Still at school	686
Y	Unemployed	2
X	Not known	14
	Total	1798

The small number shown as entering the professions is due to
the fact that those pupils who would later form the bulk of the
professions were still at school. Table 22 shows the 1961
occupations of the group classified by sex.

Of those in employment, 47 per cent of the girls but only 12
per cent of the boys were in non-manual occupations. It must
be remembered, however, that many of these posts were clerical,

which tend to be filled by females rather than males. Similarly, 44 per cent of the boys were in skilled manual occupations compared with only 11 per cent of the girls.

A fuller analysis of job choice is given later in this chapter, where the relationships between job preference while still at school, actual occupation entered after leaving school and father's occupation are investigated.

TABLE 22

OCCUPATIONS OF BOYS AND GIRLS IN 1961

Occupation		Number of Boys	Girls
School		334	352
Full-time further education		91	69
Professional or non-manual		66	191
Skilled manual		234	43
Semi-skilled manual		169	89
Factory work		21	73
Unskilled or unemployed		45	7
Not known		13	1
	Totals	973	825

In chapter 6 it was noted that the pupils at 15 appeared to have a clear appreciation of their abilities and this was reflected in their job preference at that age, the more able tending to prefer the professional and non-manual occupations.

A comparison of the scores in arithmetic and English obtained in 1960 by the various occupational sub-groups who were re-tested shows that a similar relationship existed between level of attainment and actual occupation. Table 23 gives a summary of the data.

The usual analysis revealed significant differences in level of attainments among the various occupational sub-groups, the results for both tests being very similar. The attainments of those still at school were significantly higher (in the statistical sense) than those of any other category except the professional and higher non-manual; the attainments of those in the lower non-manual group were significantly higher than those of the manual workers; and the attainments of both skilled and semi-skilled workers were significantly higher than those of the un-skilled workers.

There was therefore a strong association between level of attainment as measured by the 1960 tests, and the actual occupation entered by the young people in 1961. In general, the higher-scoring pupils remained at school or entered non-manual occupations. This is shown diagrammatically for English in figure 8. The figures from which it is derived are in Appendix E, table 93.

TABLE 23

RELATION BETWEEN 1961 OCCUPATION AND 1960 SCORE

	Arithmetic		English		Composition	
1961 occupation	Mean score	Percentile	Mean score	Percentile	Mean score	Percentile
Still at school	47·0	83	47·0	84	6·5	73
Professional and higher non-manual	39·1	67	42·1	74	6·0	72
Lower non-manual	37·9	65	36·5	60	5·3	60
Full-time further education	34·4	56	35·2	57	5·2	58
Skilled manual	30·8	47	29·3	43	4·5	41
Semi-skilled manual	29·3	44	28·0	39	4·2	38
Factory, unskilled and unemployed	23·9	31	24·1	30	3·8	36
Unknown	35·6	59	30·6	46	4·4	40

The Brunton Report (para 40) makes the point that 'selection varies in efficiency from one industry to another, in some instances it is more or less systematic, while in others it appears to be quite haphazard'. The figure and tables show that entrants to skilled manual occupations ranged in English attainments from about the 90th percentile down to the 10th and below. The range in arithmetic was equally wide. The figures in Appendix E, tables 92 and 93, are summarised in table 24 to show the calibre of the entrants in 1960–61 to skilled manual occupations and to semi-skilled, unskilled or factory work.

They show that most of the 277 entrants to skilled manual work could have been drawn from those with scores above the 50th percentile level, which appears to be acceptable to employers. If the level of acceptability is lowered to P43 or P44 a total of 274 young people (in English) or 315 (in arithmetic) was available.

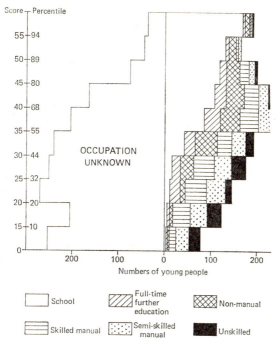

FIGURE 8   Occupation in 1961 at different levels of 1960 score in English

TABLE 24

ATTAINMENTS OF ENTRANTS TO INDUSTRY

			Number of entrants
		Occupation	
English score	*Skilled manual*	*Semi-skilled and unskilled*	*Total*
Above P55	93	99	192
Between P43 and P55	36	46	82
Below P43	142	246	388
Unknown	6	13	19
Totals	277	404	681
Arithmetic score			
Above P57	107	117	224
Between P44 and P57	38	53	91
Below P44	126	220	346
Unknown	6	14	20
Totals	277	404	681

This is undoubtedly a gross over-simplification of the position, as some of the young people with the higher scores no doubt preferred to work in semi-skilled or unskilled jobs, or were not located in the areas where the skilled work was available. Nevertheless, the fact that of the 192 entrants above the P55 level in English only 93 entered skilled manual work, while 99 entered semi-skilled or unskilled work, seems to indicate that there was some leeway to be made up in selection or guidance procedures.

OCCUPATION IN 1960–61 AND ITS RELATION TO JOB PREFERENCE 1960

At the first stage of testing in 1960 the young people were asked to indicate the job they would prefer when they were grown-up. For those who were re-tested in 1961 it was possible therefore to compare the aspirations of the previous year (1960)

TABLE 25

RELATION BETWEEN JOB PREFERRED IN 1960 AND ACTUAL OCCUPATION IN 1961

Numbers of boys

Job preferred 1960 (*Code on p 95*)

Actual occupation 1961	8	7	6	5	4	3	2	Unknown	Total
0 School	193	36	15	47	10			33	334
1 Full-time further education	8	7	1	61	6			8	91
8 and 7 Professional and higher non-manual	1	1		1				1	4
6 Lower non-manual	5	6	18	23	4			6	62
5 Skilled manual	7	11	7	171	19	1	1	17	234
4 Semi-skilled manual	4	6	14	90	42		1	12	169
3 Factory	1	1	3	9	1	5		1	21
2 Unskilled	1	1	3	21	12		2	4	44
Unemployed				1					1
Unknown	4	2		6	1				13
Totals	224	71	61	430	95	6	4	82	973

with the actual occupation taken up in 1961. Tables 25 and 26 show this comparison for boys and girls separately, using the coding system for occupations and preferences described previously in chapter 6.

One feature of the tables is the small number of boys and girls who entered the professions or higher non-manual occupations in 1961. The reason for this is, of course, that most of those proposing to enter these occupational groups continued their studies at school.

Almost half of the boys (47 per cent) entered occupations in line with their preferences of 1960 but another 40 per cent were unable in the first year of their employment to achieve their

TABLE 26

RELATION BETWEEN JOB PREFERRED IN 1960 AND ACTUAL
OCCUPATION IN 1961

Numbers of girls

		Job preferred 1960								
Actual occupation 1961	*8*	*7*	*6*	*5*	*4*	*3*	*2*	*Unknown*	*Total*
0 School	206	71	22	15	4				34	352
1 Full-time further education	12	40	12	2	2				1	69
8 and 7 Professional and higher non-manual	1	19	2	2					2	26
6 Lower non-manual	16	49	65	18	9	2			6	165
5 Skilled manual		2	6	28	2		1		4	43
4 Semi-skilled manual	7	3	11	31	26	2	2		7	89
3 Factory	2	2	4	22	27	11	2		3	73
2 Unskilled	1			3	1		1			6
Unemployed		1								1
Unknown				1						1
Totals	245	187	122	122	71	15	6	57	825

ambitions and took up employment in a different category from that in which they hoped to be when grown-up. For example, the great majority of those who had hoped to enter the professions or non-manual occupations but had left school usually found employment in the skilled or semi-skilled trades. Similarly 38 per cent of those who had hoped to enter a skilled trade had taken up less skilled employment, mainly at a semi-skilled level (28 per cent) although a small proportion (7 per cent) were in unskilled occupations. On the other hand 10 per cent of the group, mainly those preferring skilled work, entered lower non-manual occupations while some of those preferring semi-skilled work took up skilled employment.

The girls exhibited similar characteristics to the boys as regards occupational choice. Thirty-nine per cent achieved their ambitions, and 11 per cent obtained more higher skilled work. There are some differences, however, in that those who hoped to enter the professions or higher non-manual occupations usually found employment in the lower non-manual occupations, rather than the skilled and semi-skilled trades.

If we make the rather sweeping assumption that the categories of occupations can be treated as a status scale, we can estimate the extent to which the young people exceeded or fell short of their ambitions. In table 27 the difference in category levels between job preference in 1960 and actual occupation in 1961 has been used as a coarse measure of the degree to which the young person failed to realise his or her level of aspiration.

TABLE 27

EXTENT OF DIVERGENCE BETWEEN JOB PREFERENCE 1960 AND
ACTUAL OCCUPATION 1961

| | | | *Change in category levels* | | | | | | | |
| | *Downwards* | | | | | *Unchanged* | | *Upwards* | | |
	6	*5*	*4*	*3*	*2*	*1*	*0*	*1*	*2*	*3*	*Total*
Boys	1	2	8	37	51	104	240	42	6	2	493
Girls	1	2	9	10	52	114	150	25	14	3	380
Totals	2	4	17	47	103	218	390	67	20	5	873

For example, the number of boys falling short of their original job preference by one category was 104 whereas the number who exceeded their original job preference by one category was 42.

The number in the group who exceeded their 1960 level of aspiration by more than one category was very small and this confirms what has been said in the previous paragraphs. The variations among those who failed to reach their 1960 levels of aspiration were greater, substantial proportions falling two or three category levels, and some, five or six. Nevertheless, as table 27 shows, 77 per cent of the group either realised their occupational ambitions or were very close to it (being one category above or below).

The age of 16 is much too early in the young person's life for the research worker to say whether the young people were able to fulfil their aspirations but it would appear from the data that most of them were on the way to doing so.

RELATION BETWEEN JOB PREFERENCE IN 1960 AND THAT
IN 1961

The question may be raised 'How stable is the preference
expressed by young people at the age of 15?' We have a little
information on this subject, since the questionnaires used in
1961, when the young people were nearing 16, asked what job
each would like to have at the age of 21. The fact that the item
appeared under the general heading 'Work' was unfortunate,
since replies were not given by many of those still at school.
The results of the comparison between the 1960 and the 1961
replies for the group who attended for testing in 1961 are given
in table 28, in which the frequencies showing unchanged
preferences have been shown in bold type.

TABLE 28

RELATION BETWEEN JOB PREFERRED IN 1960 AND JOB PREFERRED IN 1961

| | | | | Job preferred in 1960 (Code as for 1961) | | | | | |
Job preferred in 1961	8	7	6	5	4	3	2	X	Total
8 Professional	**232**	22	9	33	12	2	1	35	346
7 Higher non-manual	35	**150**	40	31	13	1		16	286
6 Lower non-manual	11	22	**69**	29	8	2		13	154
5 Skilled manual	27	21	23	**319**	40	3	4	21	458
4 Semi-skilled manual	3	5	8	66	**58**		2	14	156
3 Factory			2	3	14	**8**	1	2	30
2 Unskilled	1	1	1	5	4		**1**		13
X Not known	160	37	31	66	17	5	1	38	355
Totals	469	258	183	552	166	21	10	139	1798

Of the 1342 for whom job preferences are known for both
1960 and 1961, no fewer than 837, ie 62 per cent, gave the same
preference. If the pupils still at school in 1961 had added their
responses this percentage would doubtless have been still
higher. Within the rough categories used for coding the responses the preferences of the majority of the young people
were relatively stable within the 10-month period between the
two surveys.

For the few large discrepancies between 1960 and 1961 preferences there are sometimes simple explanations. The girl
whose preferred occupation changed from 8 to 2 was a low
scorer in both tests on both occasions. She indicated in 1960

that she hoped to be a nurse (coded as a minor profession) but in 1961 changed it to 'children's nurse', which was coded as a domestic occupation. She was, in 1961, a shop assistant and was not attending evening classes. The girl whose preference changed in the reverse direction, from 2 to 8, gave domestic work as her choice in 1960, was engaged as a nursery nurse, and in 1961 hoped to become a nursery class teacher. One girl whose preference in 1960 was for factory work (category 3) obtained employment in a factory and in 1961 stated her wish to be a gymnastic instructor (category 8) when 21.

OCCUPATION IN 1960–61 AND ITS RELATION TO FATHER'S OCCUPATION

We have already seen that the occupation in 1960–61 was closely related to the scores in the 1960 tests. It may be that it was also related to the occupation of the father, all of these variables tending to be interlinked with each other. Separate analyses were made for boys and girls and the results are shown

TABLE 29

RELATION BETWEEN OCCUPATION 1960–61 AND FATHER'S OCCUPATION

Numbers of boys

Occupation 1960–61

Father's occupation	0	1	8, 7, 6	5	4	3, 2	X	Total
Major professional	57	2	1		3	1		64
Minor professional	15	3	2	4	7	1	1	33
Higher non-manual	31	6	2	4	6			49
Lower non-manual	56	11	12	25	15	2	1	122
Skilled manual	75	24	23	65	39	15	2	243
Semi-skilled manual	47	26	11	67	53	21	5	230
Unskilled manual	16	5	7	27	16	8	1	80
Agriculture	12	3	2	11	15	2	1	46
Unemployed		4	1		2	4		11
Father dead	17	4	2	23	11	4	1	62
Unknown	8	3	3	8	2	7	1	32
Totals	334	91	66	234	169	65	13	972

in tables 29 and 30. The coding for occupations 1960–61 is given on page 57. The one unemployed boy and the one unemployed girl have been omitted. To assist the reader in scanning these tables the largest figure in each row has been shown in bold type (except where there are several maxima).

The trend is unmistakable in each table. The sons and daughters of the professional and non-manual workers and of the skilled manual workers tended to remain at school for at least a further year. Where there was no father, or the father's occupation was in agriculture, this was also true for the girls but not for the boys.

TABLE 30

RELATION BETWEEN OCCUPATION 1960–61 AND FATHER'S OCCUPATION

| | | | | | | | | Numbers of girls |
| | | | Occupation 1960–61 | | | | | |
Father's occupation	0	1	8, 7, 6	5	4	3, 2	X	Total
Major professional	**41**	7	3					51
Minor professional	**18**	2	5	1		2		28
Higher non-manual	**39**	4	6	2	4	1		56
Lower non-manual	**63**	7	16	8	8	1	1	104
Skilled manual	**81**	17	70	5	25	12		210
Semi-skilled manual	43	15	**53**	16	26	29		182
Unskilled manual	8	4	14	5	12	**16**		59
Agriculture	**26**	5	2	2	8	3		46
Unemployed	1	1	2	1	1	**3**		9
Father dead	**27**	6	12	2	4	6		57
Unknown	5	1	**8**	1	1	6		22
Totals	352	69	191	43	89	79	1	824

When this has been said, and the columns headed 0 (school) and 1 (full-time further education) are no longer under consideration, there are no strong associations in the boys' table and few in the girls' table. In the latter, it may be observed that the daughters of the skilled manual workers who did enter employment favoured non-manual work, while the daughters of unskilled or unemployed workers favoured factory or unskilled work. This type of work was shunned by the daughters of the professional and non-manual workers.

As has been previously said, the age of 16 is too early in the young person's life for final conclusions to be drawn on the relation of occupation to other factors, but it does appear that the main influence of father's occupation is over the decision whether to continue in full-time education and that otherwise there is little association between the occupation of the young person and that of his father.

TYPE OF EDUCATION IN 1960–61 AND ITS RELATION TO 1960 SCORES

The young people were classified into the following categories according to the type of education they had undertaken in the year subsequent to the first testing.

Code No	Description of category	No
8	In senior secondary courses	577
7	In junior secondary courses	109
6	In full-time further education	160
5	Attending day-release classes	136
4	Attending part-time evening vocational classes	346
3	Attending part-time evening non-vocational classes	22
2	Not attending classes	436
X	No information available	12
	Total	1798

Of the group, 686 were still at school; of these 577 (84 per cent) were following senior secondary courses and 109 (16 per cent) were in junior secondary courses. A further 160 young people were engaged in full-time further education. Table 31 shows the distribution by sex of those continuing in full-time education.

TABLE 31

FULL-TIME EDUCATION COURSE BY SEX

	Sex		
Type of course	Boys	Girls	Total
Senior secondary	288	289	577
Junior secondary	46	63	109
Further education	91	69	160
Totals	425	421	846

There was no association between sex and type of course.

Tables 32 and 33 show the type of further education undertaken by the 537 boys and 403 girls who were known to have entered employment. (The two unemployed have been included.) The data show clearly the association between further study and type of employment. The higher the status of the job, the more likely was it that the young person concerned was continuing to study after leaving school, eg 74 per cent of the girls in non-manual occupations were taking further education classes compared with 21 per cent of the girls in unskilled employment.

Two other points of importance emerge. Firstly, there is the small proportion of girls obtaining day-release from their

TABLE 32

TYPE OF PART-TIME FURTHER EDUCATION AND OCCUPATION 1960–61

Numbers and percentages of boys
Type of further education
Evening

Present occupation	*Day-release*	*Vocational*	*Non-vocational*	*None*	*Total*
Professional or non-manual	7 (11)	35 (53)		24 (36)	66 (100)
Skilled manual	75 (32)	84 (36)	2 (1)	73 (31)	234 (100)
Semi-skilled manual	33 (20)	40 (24)	5 (3)	91 (54)	169 (100)
Unskilled or un-employed	4 (6)	8 (12)	2 (3)	52 (79)	66 (100)
Unknown				2	2
Totals	119 (22)	167 (31)	9 (2)	242 (45)	537 (100)

TABLE 33

TYPE OF PART-TIME FURTHER EDUCATION AND OCCUPATION 1960–61

Numbers and percentages of girls
Type of further education
Evening

Present occupation	*Day-release*	*Vocational*	*Non-vocational*	*None*	*Total*
Professional or non-manual	2 (1)	135 (71)	5 (3)	49 (26)	191 (100)
Skilled manual	10 (23)	13 (30)	3 (7)	17 (40)	43 (100)
Shops	2 (2)	20 (23)	2 (2)	65 (73)	89 (100)
Unskilled or un-employed	3 (4)	11 (14)	3 (4)	63 (79)	80 (100)
Totals	17 (4)	179 (44)	13 (3)	194 (48)	403 (100)

employers to undertake further study. Only 4 per cent of the girls compared with 22 per cent of the boys were taking day-release classes, and those who did were mainly following skilled trades. For girls in non-manual employment, shops, factories and unskilled jobs, the proportion who obtained day-release was very small indeed.

These figures reinforce the comments made in the Brunton Report—'disappointingly few young workers are granted day-release by their employers for day-time study'. 'Employers are often unwilling to incur expenditure on the training of girls which will not yield a full return before the girls leave on marrying or shortly after marriage.'[1]   Secondly, a high proportion of boys and girls in non-manual occupations were studying by means of evening classes.   Eighty-three per cent of the boys and 99 per cent of the girls in this occupational category who were taking further education courses did so by means of evening classes rather than by the day-release system. Whether these young people were forced to take evening classes because the appropriate classes were not available during the day, or because their employers refused to grant them day-release is not known.

The Brunton Report makes it clear that 'there are still employers who are content to encourage their young employees to attend evening classes when suitable day classes are available'. Certainly both sets of circumstances are possible and operate in practice, but it is unfortunate that, where the desire to study is so apparent, provision should not be made to enable the young people to study during the day rather than in the evening.

The general picture is one in which just over half of these in employment and for whom information was available were taking some form of further education.   Of these, practically all the girls and a large majority of the boys were studying part-time in the evening.   Only for those in the skilled manual or semi-skilled manual occupations was there an appreciable measure of study by the day-release system.

Are there differences in general level of attainment in the students taking different types of further education?   To answer this question it is necessary to relate the 1960 scores in English and arithmetic to the type of education undertaken by the young worker in 1961.   Table 34 gives a summary of the relevant data.

The usual analysis revealed significant differences in level of attainment among the various categories and the results for both tests were very similar.   When the categories with small

[1] pp 6, 14.

TABLE 34

RELATIONSHIP BETWEEN TYPE OF EDUCATION IN 1961
AND SCORES IN 1960 TESTS

| | *1960 Mean Scores* | | | | | |
| | Arithmetic | | | English | | |
Type of Education 1961	*Score*	*Percentile*	*No*	*Score*	*Percentile*	*No*
Senior secondary course	48·8	85	564	49·0	87	577
Junior secondary course	37·5	64	109	36·2	60	108
Full-time further education	34·4	56	156	35·2	57	155
Part-time day-release classes	33·4	54	130	31·7	48	133
Part-time evening vocational classes	33·7	54	341	32·4	50	339
Part-time evening non-vocational classes	30·9	47	22	29·5	43	22
None	28·8	42	425	28·2	40	421
Not known	37·8	64	12	30·8	46	12
Absent from 1960 tests			39			31
Totals			1798			1798

numbers (fewer than 25) were omitted, the remainder could be classified into separate strata in descending order of attainment in the tests as follows:

(*a*) senior secondary course
(*b*) junior secondary course
    full-time further education
    day-release classes
    part-time evening vocational classes
(*c*) none

The higher attainment of those remaining in full-time education at school has already been established on page 102. The present results serve to reinforce this conclusion and also reveal that those of the group who entered the further education system were the better equipped of those who left school and went into employment. The difficulties of obtaining day-release for study purposes from certain occupations have already been mentioned and the figures in table 34 indicate that there is no real difference in general level of initial attainment between

8

those studying by day-release and by evening classes. Furthermore, tables 32 and 33 indicate that the absentees from further education were not confined only to the unskilled occupations, but came also from the skilled, semi-skilled, and non-manual occupations.

It would have been of interest to know why these young people did not enter the further education system, but unfortunately this information was not obtained.

RELATION BETWEEN TYPE OF EDUCATION AND FATHER'S OCCUPATION

Tables 35 and 36 show the type of education undertaken in 1960–61 by the boys and girls in the groups classified by father's occupation. The highest frequencies in each row are printed in bold type.

TABLE 35

RELATION BETWEEN TYPE OF EDUCATION 1960–61 AND FATHER'S OCCUPATION

Numbers of boys

Type of education

Father's occupation	Sen sec	Jun sec	Full-time FE	Day-release	Evening voc	Evening non-voc	None	Not known	Total
Major professional	**56**	1	2	2			2		64
Minor professional	**13**	2	3	3	4		7	1	33
Higher non-manual	**26**	5	6		5	2	5		49
Lower non-manual	**46**	10	11	10	28		16	1	122
Skilled manual	**68**	7	24	36	57	3	46	2	243
Semi-skilled manual	34	13	26	37	40	3	**74**	4	231
Unskilled	14	2	5	8	8		**43**		80
Agriculture	9	3	3	3	5		**22**	1	46
Unemployed			4	1		1	**5**		11
Father dead	15	2	4	14	11		**15**	1	62
Unknown	7	1	3	5	8		7	1	32
Totals	288	46	91	119	167	9	242	11	973

An analysis revealed a significant association between the two variables. A further examination of the data indicated that the significance of the association was due mainly to the contributions from the 'Senior Secondary' and 'None' and 'Non-vocational' sub-categories. The analysis was therefore repeated with these sub-categories omitted from the tables when the value of chi-square (the degree of association) was found to be non-significant for the girls and just significant at the 5 per cent level for boys. The conclusion can therefore be drawn that father's occupation is related to whether the young person

TABLE 36

RELATION BETWEEN TYPE OF EDUCATION AND FATHER'S OCCUPATION

Numbers of girls

Type of education

Father's occupation	Sen sec	Jun sec	Full-time FE	Day-release	Evening voc	Evening non-voc	None	Not known	Total
Major professional	39	2	7		3				51
Minor professional	14	4	2	1	4		3		28
Higher non-manual	34	5	4		5	1	7		56
Lower non-manual	57	6	7	2	17		14	1	104
Skilled manual	65	16	17	2	63	4	44		211
Semi-skilled	31	12	15	7	50	4	63		182
Unskilled	6	2	4	2	17		28		59
Agriculture	20	6	5	1	2	1	11		46
Unemployed	1		1		1	1	5		9
Father dead	19	8	6		10	2	12		57
Unknown	3	2	1	2	7		7		22
Totals	289	63	69	17	179	13	194	1	825

continues to follow a senior secondary course if he remains at school and also to whether the young person does not take any further education course of a vocational nature if he has left school. Otherwise it appears to have little bearing on the type of further education actually taken up by those young people who have left school.

Table 37 shows the percentages of the young people (boys and girls combined) (*a*) remaining in senior secondary courses, and (*b*) taking no vocational courses in further education for each category of father's occupation. Sixty-five per cent of the children of professional and self-employed men continued their academic course of study at school while only 9 per cent failed to take a vocational course of some description. On the other hand, 51 per cent of the children of unskilled workers were not following any vocational course of education and only 17 per cent remained at school in senior secondary courses. Table 37

TABLE 37

PERCENTAGES OF EACH OCCUPATIONAL CATEGORY
(a) REMAINING IN SENIOR SECONDARY COURSES
(b) TAKING NO VOCATIONAL FURTHER EDUCATION CLASSES

| | Father's occupation | | | | | |
	Professional and self-employed	Non-manual	Skilled manual	Semi-skilled manual	Unskilled manual	Not known
(a) Remaining in senior secondary courses	65	50	29	16	17	26
(b) Taking no vocational FE classes	9	14	21	35	51	25

shows clearly the differences between the various occupational categories.

The higher the occupational status of the father, the more likely is it that the young person will continue his education, whether at school or in employment.

LEISURE ACTIVITIES

The leisure activities reported by the young people in 1961 were coded according to the scheme on next page.

The total number of activities listed (4788) exceeds the number of young people in the group (1798) since many of the group listed more than one leisure activity. Table 38 shows the number of young people undertaking a particular number of leisure activities. In this table X indicates the number of young people who failed to answer this part of the questionnaire. The majority of the group (56 per cent) took part in two or three activities, while only 2 per cent indicated that they had no leisure pursuits.

Tables 39 and 40 show the distribution of leisure pursuits by sex and by present occupation. To simplify the presentation of the data, some telescoping of the categories shown on page 117 has been carried out, eg, the original codes 89 and 88 have been

Code No	Type of leisure activity	No in category
90	Youth leadership or voluntary service to others	36
89	Music—playing instrument, singing	90
88	Music—listening to records	131
77	Theatre—active dramatic work	16
76	Theatre—passive attendance	3
65	Games and sports—active	864
64	Games and sports—indoor active	619
63	Games and sports—spectator	80
50	Hobbies	457
40	TV	210
30	Cinema, radio, variety theatre	329
20	Dancing	412
12	Visiting and going out with friends	35
11	Visiting cafés	29
00	Reading	589
XX	None stated	61
XO	Activities listed under youth organisation	823
YY	Unclassified	4
	Total	4788

combined in one code 8, and codes 77 and 76 appear as code 7. A similar procedure was adopted for the other categories.

TABLE 38

NUMBER OF LEISURE ACTIVITIES REPORTED

Number of activities	0	1	2	3	4	5	6 and over	x	Total
Number of young people	35	26	513	501	279	110	37	27	1798
Percentage of group	2	16	29	28	16	6	2	2	100

TABLE 39

NUMBERS OF BOYS IN EACH OCCUPATION ENGAGING IN
DIFFERENT LEISURE ACTIVITIES

Code number of leisure activity

Present occupation	9	8,7	6	5	4	3	2	1	0	X	Y	No in occupation
Professional and non-manual	0	6	52	12	8	9	10	1	15	41		66
Skilled manual	3	18	162	34	16	33	49	5	21	131		234
Semi-skilled manual	0	8	126	27	13	38	20	6	30	60		169
Unskilled and unemployed	1	1	38	14	5	19	13	4	12	23		66
Full-time further education	0	11	69	26	13	12	7	2	19	48		91
School	5	44	259	85	29	29	22	15	118	187	2	334
Not known			1							12		13
Total	9	88	707	198	84	140	121	33	215	502	2	973
Percentage of group	1		74	21	9	15	13	3	22	51		100

In general, the girls in the group took more part in leisure activities than did the boys. The exception was games where 74 per cent of the boys were involved compared with 57 per cent of the girls.

The order of popularity of the various leisure activities was similar for both boys and girls. Games and sports, reading, hobbies and dancing enjoyed the greatest support. The more

TABLE 40

NUMBERS OF GIRLS IN EACH OCCUPATION ENGAGING IN
DIFFERENT LEISURE ACTIVITIES

Code number of leisure activity

Present occupation	9	8,7	6	5	4	3	2	1	0	X	Y	No in occupation
Professional and non-manual	6	40	107	63	23	57	106	5	65	92		191
Skilled manual	1	5	22	12	6	8	20	3	11	22		43
Shops	0	9	29	29	15	29	32	6	24	24		89
Factory, unskilled and unemployed	1	6	23	21	16	24	32	2	18	19	1	80
Full-time further education	2	9	50	19	18	13	22	5	38	34		69
School	17	73	238	115	48	58	79	7	218	192	1	352
Not known										1		1
Total	27	142	469	259	126	189	291	28	374	384	2	825
Percentage of group	3	17	57	31	15	23	35	3	45	47		100

cultural pursuits, such as the theatre and music, were not popular. Only five boys and fourteen girls indicated an interest in the theatre, while 5 per cent of the whole group played a musical instrument or sang and 7 per cent listened to records. Furthermore, these two activities were followed mainly by those still at school or in non-manual occupations.

The proportion of boys taking part in games and sports was uniformly high, no matter the occupation being followed, but the proportion was high for those girls who were in full-time education (69 per cent) and was low for those in shops and unskilled jobs (31 per cent).

Although reading was the second most popular leisure pursuit in the group as a whole, it was much more a pursuit of those still at school or in full-time further education, (47 per cent), than of those in employment (21 per cent). Hobbies were also associated with the continuance of full-time education (26 per cent) rather than with employment (16 per cent) in the case of the boys. Dancing, on the other hand, was associated with employment rather than with continuing education and was much more popular with the girls in the group than with the boys. Of those in employment, 47 per cent of the girls but only 17 per cent of the boys indicated an interest in dancing.

Despite these differences there was considerable agreement among the various occupational sub-groups as to the popularity of the various activities. One way of measuring the amount of agreement is to calculate Kendall's Coefficient of Concordance (W). This coefficient has a value between zero (indicating no agreement) and 1 (indicating complete agreement). W was calculated for the girls and boys separately, and also for the two sexes taken together. The values of W obtained were relatively high indicating a good measure of agreement among the occupational sub-groups. They were for boys 0·83, for girls 0·87, and for boys and girls together 0·81, indicating a general agreement between the sexes on the popularity of the various activities.

YOUTH ORGANISATIONS

The youth organisations to which the young people belonged were coded according to the scheme shown below. Some of the group belonged to more than one organisation and the total of the category numbers (1887) therefore exceeds the actual number of young people involved (1798).

Code No	Type of youth organisation	No in category
8	Scouts or Guides	193
7	Boys' Brigade, Girls' Guildry, Girls' Life Brigade	136
6	Pre-service organisations	47
5	Political organisations	11
4	Church Clubs	226
3	Youth Clubs other than Church Clubs	221
2	Athletic Clubs	57
1	Outdoor but not strictly athletic	25
0	None	919
X	Not classified or not known	52

A further analysis of the data was made on the basis of sex and present occupation. Tables 41 and 42 show the distribution of youth organisations by sex and occupation.

Just over half of the group (51 per cent) did not belong to any youth organisation. The tendency to non-membership was more prevalent among the young people in semi-skilled and unskilled jobs (70 per cent) than among those who were in other occupations or remained at school (47 per cent).

TABLE 41

NUMBERS OF BOYS IN EACH OCCUPATION AND YOUTH ORGANISATION

Code number of organisation

Present occupation	8	7	6, 5	4	3	2, 1	0	X	No in occupation
Professional and non-manual	3	18	3	9	10	1	26		66
Skilled manual	17	33	17	18	34	12	112	2	234
Semi-skilled manual	10	12	6	6	23	4	108	1	169
Unskilled and unemployed	1	8	3	3	6	5	42		66
Full-time further education	7	11	4	11	10	11	41	3	91
School	66	35	17	34	22	18	148	15	334
Unknown							2	11	13
Totals	104	117	50	81	105	51	479	32	973
Percentage of group	11	12	5	8	11	5	49	3	100

TABLE 42

NUMBERS OF GIRLS IN EACH OCCUPATION AND YOUTH ORGANISATION

Code number of organisation

Present occupation	8	7, 6, 5	4	3	2, 1	0	X	No in occupation
Professional and non-manual	15	7	31	48	5	98		191
Skilled manual	1	1	8	11	1	22		43
Shops	2	2	9	5	2	68	1	89
Factory, unskilled and unemployed	2	0	5	9	0	64		80
Full-time further education	4	0	17	14	1	35	1	69
School	65	17	75	29	22	153	17	352
Unknown							1	1
Totals	89	27	145	116	31	440	20	825
Percentage of group	11	3	18	14	4	53	2	100

For those who were members of youth organisations the most popular were the church clubs (27 per cent), youth clubs (27 per cent), Boys' Brigade (25 per cent) and the Scouts or Guides (23 per cent). The Scouts and Guides were activities followed mainly by those still at school, only 6 per cent of those who had left school being members, compared with 20 per cent of those at school. The church clubs and youth clubs were more popular with the girls than the boys. Those girls still in full-time education tended to belong to the church clubs (23 per cent), while those in employment took more part in the other youth clubs (24 per cent). The corresponding figures for the boys were 11 and 14 per cent.

Membership of the pre-service and political organisations was relatively small (3 per cent) and almost exclusively male, while some 5 per cent of the group were members of athletic clubs or other outdoor clubs.

Apart from the differences mentioned above, type of occupation and sex were found to bear little relationship to the youth organisations to which the group belonged.

NEWSPAPERS READ

The newspapers read by the young people were coded according to the following scheme; where several newspapers were mentioned, that with the highest coding was recorded.

Code No	Newspaper	No of readers
8	Scotsman, Guardian, The Times, Glasgow Herald, Daily Telegraph, Daily Mail, Daily Express, Daily Herald	204
7	Daily Record, Daily Mirror	1225
6	Evening News, Dispatch, Evening Times, Citizen, local paper	182
5	Sunday paper	40
4	Other paper	10
0	None	79
X	Not stated or unclassifiable	58
	Total	1798

For example, the figure of 40 for Sunday papers indicated that these young people read Sunday papers but none of those classified under codes 6 to 8. It should perhaps be stated that the coding was used only as a principle of classification and not as a measure of the excellence of the newspapers.

About 90 per cent of the group claimed that they read regularly some daily newspaper; of these 11 per cent read the newspapers coded 8; 68 per cent the morning dailies coded 7, and 10 per cent evening papers coded 6. Only 4 per cent stated that they read no paper at all.

Since the newspapers which entered the home was likely to be determined by the parents of the young person rather than the young person himself, no further analysis of the data was made at this stage.

LAST BOOK READ AND ITS RELATION TO OCCUPATION AND TO 1960 SCORES

In order to assess the reading habits of the group, the young people were asked for information about the last book they had read. The information obtained was coded as shown:

Code No	Description of book	No in category
7	Traditional classic	135
6	Modern novel	184
5	Technical, recreational, travel or other non-fiction	385
4	Popular fiction, eg, school story	296
3	Popular fiction, eg, thriller	73
2	No book read since school persuasion ceased, or, if still at school, except by persuasion	328
1	Silly or dishonest answer	25
0	No answer given	336
X	Unclassifiable	36
	Total	1798

Tables 43 and 44 show the distribution of books read, by sex and by present occupation. Analysis of the data on the basis of

TABLE 43

RELATION BETWEEN OCCUPATION AND LAST BOOK READ

Numbers of boys

Present occupation	Code number of last book read							No in occupation
	7	6	5	4, 3	2, 3	0	X	
Professional and non-manual	4	7	16	12	16	11		66
Skilled manual	1	9	78	43	44	58	1	234
Semi-skilled manual	4	4	43	27	35	54	2	169
Unskilled and unemployed	0	0	14	16	14	22		66
Full-time further education	1	7	32	30	5	16		91
School	38	61	97	54	57	17	10	334
Unknown			1			1	11	13
Totals	48	88	281	182	171	179	24	973
Percentages	5	9	29	19	18	18	2	100

sex and present occupation revealed no significant relationship between type of employment and type of book read. Nor were there any great differences between the sexes, with the exception of the non-fiction books coded under 5. This category of book was named by 29 per cent of the boys but by only 13 per cent of the girls.

The major difference in reading habits was between those of the group who continued at school and those who went into employment. Of the 135 young people who indicated they read some of the 'classics', only 21 were not still at school. A similar, though less extreme, position was found as regards the

TABLE 44

RELATION BETWEEN OCCUPATION AND LAST BOOK READ

Numbers of girls

| | Code number of last book read | | | | | | | No in |
Present occupation	8, 7	6	5	4, 3	2, 1	0	X	occupation
Professional and								
non-manual	4	12	21	63	41	50		191
Skilled manual	2	4	9	10	5	13		43
Shops	0	3	9	20	22	35		89
Factory, unskilled,								
and unemployed	2	1	6	16	22	33		80
Full-time further								
education	3	10	12	16	18	10		69
School	76	66	47	62	74	16	11	352
Unknown							1	1
Totals	87	96	104	187	182	157	12	825
Percentages	11	12	13	23	22	19	1	100

modern novel; of the 184 in the group who were in this category, 127 were still at school. It would appear that once the young people leave school they retain little enthusiasm for serious literature. This lack of interest is confirmed by the fact that 18 per cent of the group stated they had either not read any book since leaving school or, though still at school, had read only under persuasion. When one considers that a further 19 per cent (most of whom were in employment) gave no answer to the question, it would seem that over one-third of the group read very little literature of any description, serious or otherwise.

Were the reading habits of the group related to their general level of attainment in the 1960 tests? To answer this question, comparisons were made of the average scores obtained in English and arithmetic in 1960 by those favouring the various categories of 'book read'. Table 45 gives a summary of the data.

TABLE 45

RELATIONSHIP BETWEEN 1960 SCORES AND BOOKS READ

| | 1960 *Scores of readers* | | | |
| | Arithmetic | | English | |
Category of book read	*Mean score*	*Percentile*	*Mean score*	*Percentile*
7	46·4	82	47·7	85
6	45·6	81	46·0	83
5	37·5	64	37·0	61
4	37·4	63	37·3	62
3	36·3	61	35·6	58
2	38·1	65	38·1	64
1	30·8	47	28·0	39
0	29·7	44	28·1	39
X	43·9	78	38·0	64

The usual analysis revealed significant differences among the various categories of books read, the results for both tests being very similar. Using the English scores as a basis, it was possible to classify the various categories into distinct strata in descending order of level of attainment as follows:

(a) Categories 7 and 6 (traditional classic or modern novel)
(b) Categories 5, 4, 3, 2 and X (non-fiction, popular fiction or no book read)
(c) Categories 1 and 0 (silly or dishonest or no answer).

Categories 7 and 6 include the more serious literature. It was found that reading of this type was restricted mainly to those who continued at school, who have already been shown to be usually higher scorers than those who left school. It is therefore not surprising that the readers of books in categories 7 and 6 made higher marks than the others in the tests.

Those in categories 5, 4, 3, 2 and X read other types of literature, or, indeed, read none at all and it would appear that level of score has little relationship to general reading habits within these categories. On the other hand, failure to answer truthfully (category 1) or to give any response at all (category 0) was associated with a lower level of attainment.

SUMMARY

This chapter has attempted to cover the activities of the group between the ages of 15 and 16. Unfortunately, information was

WHAT THEY DID BETWEEN 15 AND 16   125

available for only half of the original group. The occupations entered by the young people, the type of education they followed, their leisure pursuits and reading habits have been investigated and the main findings are summarised here.

Very few members of the group entered the professions in 1960–61. This is not unexpected, since those who would later form the bulk of the professions were still at school. Almost half of the girls who left school entered the non-manual occupations, while a similar proportion of the boys took up skilled trades.

A strong association was found between level of attainment in the 1960 tests and type of occupation entered by the young person. It was clear that those who entered the non-manual and professional occupations were more proficient in the basic skills than those entering the skilled and semi-skilled trades; they in turn were superior in attainment to the factory and unskilled workers.

A further point of interest was the association between the continuance of full-time education and level of attainment. Those who remained at school, presumably with the intention of entering the professions or non-manual occupations, were of higher proficiency than those who left school to take up similar posts. The young people who entered full-time further education were superior in attainments to those taking up skilled or semi-skilled occupations. This desire on the part of the more proficient pupils to continue their education was also shown by those who entered employment. Just over half of them took some form of further education and they were superior in attainment to those who did not.

The great majority of the young people were unable to obtain day-release facilities and were obliged to study in the evening. This was particularly evident in the case of the girls, of whom only 4 per cent, compared with 22 per cent of the boys, were attending day-release classes. Again, practically all of those who entered the professions or non-manual employment and continued their education were studying in evening classes. Only for those in the skilled or semi-skilled trades was there an appreciable measure of study by the day-release system.

The occupational status of the father was found to be strongly associated with staying on at school, and also with the continuance of education, where the young person had left school. For example, 65 per cent of the children of professional and self-employed men continued their academic course of study at school, while only 9 per cent took no form of education during the year. On the other hand, 51 per cent of the children of unskilled workers were not following any educational course and only 17 per cent remained at school.

Only 2 per cent of the group indicated that they had no leisure activities, while the majority took part in two or three. Games and sports, reading, hobbies and dancing were the most popular activities. Reading and hobbies tended, however, to be much more the pursuit of those still at school or in full-time further education.

Just over half of the young people did not belong to any youth organisation. This tendency to non-participation was more prevalent among the semi-skilled and unskilled workers. For those who were members, the most popular were the church clubs and youth clubs and the uniformed organisations, like the Boys' Brigade, the Scouts and the Guides. The Scouts and Guides were mainly recruited from those still at school, only 6 per cent of those who had left school being members.

Four per cent of the group indicated that they read no newspaper during the week. The most popular papers were the large dailies, such as the *Daily Express* and the *Daily Mail*, which were read by 47 per cent of the group.

The reading habits of the group were found to be unrelated to type of employment. The reading of serious literature was restricted, mainly, to those who remained at school. Once the young people left school they seemed to have little enthusiasm for the more serious forms of literature; indeed, over one-third of them appeared to have read little of any description, serious or otherwise, since leaving school. The failure of the educational system to produce a lasting effect on the reading habits of the group must give cause for concern and would seem to require investigation.

Chapter 8

WHAT THEY RETAINED AT 16

Arrangements were made for the original group to be re-tested in March 1961, ten months after the first stage of testing. As indicated in chapter 3, there were great difficulties in making contact with some members of the 1960 group since many of them had left school in the interval and were in various occupations. Contact was made with schools, further education colleges, employers, and where necessary directly with the young person concerned in an endeavour to obtain as large a response as possible at the re-test stage. The methods used to make contact have been described fully in chapter 3. Despite these efforts only 1798 or 51 per cent of the 1960 group took the tests in 1961. Table 46 gives a break-down of the re-test group classified by test situation. There were five categories of young people involved:

(*a*) those still at school and tested there
(*b*) those attending further education centres (full-time, day-release and evening) and tested there
(*c*) those tested in employers' premises
(*d*) those released by employers and tested at convenient centres
(*e*) the remainder who were invited to attend at test centres.

The figures of table 46 show that of those still at school in 1961 almost 84 per cent were re-tested. The response from those attending further education centres was not so high (57 per cent), but it must be remembered that this figure includes evening students as well as day students.

In area 1 a relatively poor response by evening-class students was possibly due to the concentration of the re-testing in

TABLE 46

NUMBERS OF YOUNG PEOPLE ATTENDING FOR SECOND TESTING

| Area[1] | Place of Testing | | | | | | | | | | | Total | |
| | (a) | | (b) | | (c) | | (d) | | (e) | | | | |
	Actual	Possible	Actual	Possible	Actual	Possible	Actual	Possible	Actual	Possible		Actual	Possible
1	224	248	131	260	26	27	23	36	115	662		519	1233
2	73	83	32	41	12	14	18	20	60	212		195	370
3	54	60	21	32	11	12	12	12	27	90		125	206
4	252	341	248	410	30	39	107	123	147	454		784	1367
5	83	87	41	82	4	10	17	22	30	170		175	371
Totals	686	819	473	825	83	102	177	213	379	1588		1798	3547
Percentage attending	84		57		81		83		24			51	

[1] cf p 24.

seventeen centres instead of the fifty-two normally attended by the young people.

Previous mention has been made in chapter 3 of the poor response made by the employers to the Committee's appeal for their co-operation in the project. Columns (c) and (d) of table 46 show that where the employer did agree to co-operate by either releasing the employee for testing or arranging to have the testing carried out on his own premises the response of the employees was very high, being over 80 per cent. It is unfortunate from the point of view of the investigation that there were not more employers able to co-operate at the re-test stage.

The poorest response came from the 'remainder' group who could not be contacted by other methods and had to be invited by letter to attend for re-testing.

While the overall response from all who had left school was 41 per cent the response from the 'remainder' group was only 24 per cent. In an attempt to achieve a good response many of this group were visited by students from the colleges of education who explained the purpose of the re-test and encouraged them to attend a testing centre. Fifty-three of these students provided comments on their experiences; these have been collated by Mr J G Morris, a member of the Committee, and are given at the end of this chapter. Of the 1047 young people visited, 264 (just over 25 per cent) were re-tested.

The general conclusion is that where the co-operation of the young person's headteacher or employer was obtained it was possible to obtain a high response at the re-test stage but where this was lacking the response was low. The Committee considered the possibility of making further efforts to contact the non-responders but this was eventually rejected in view of the time and expense involved.

The association of a test with the 'school' situation made a number of the young people reluctant to participate. This was illustrated in one day-release class where the headmaster found two students, who were attending classes in hairdressing and attempting one of the tests, on the verge of tears. On inquiry into the cause he was given the reply 'We thought we had left all this behind when we left school and came to day-release classes'.

9

On the other hand, testing on the employer's premises was not without its hazards. One apprentice was observed to have made unusually large gains between the 1960 and 1961 tests. He had moved from the P5 to the P92 level in arithmetic, and from the P6 to the P78 level in English. Judicious inquiries revealed that the supervision arrangements at the 1961 tests had broken down and that he had been aided by his fellow craftsmen. The most striking thing about this occurrence may be the degree of excellence achieved by the combined efforts of himself and his fellow workers in the 1961 tests!

THE GAINS AND LOSSES IN THE THREE TESTS

The interest in this stage of the experiment lies less in the actual scores made by the young people who returned for the second set of tests than in the gains or losses each made in the

TABLE 47

DISTRIBUTION OF GAINS AND LOSSES IN EACH OF THE THREE TESTS

Gain in score	Frequency of gain Arithmetic	English	Gain in score	Frequency of gain Composition
			6	2
			5	12
23 to 27	0	1	4	35
18 to 22	21	6	3	81
13 to 17	109	56	2	269
8 to 12	237	239	1	238
3 to 7	392	564	0	546
−2 to 2	462	530	−1	232
−7 to −3	312	283	−2	214
−12 to −8	151	60	−3	76
−17 to −13	46	12	−4	24
−22 to −18	8	0	−5	11
			−6	0
			−7	1
Not known	60	47		57
Total number	1798	1798		1798
Mean gain	1·4	2·3		0·11
Standard deviation of gains	7·55	5·85		1·77

tests and in the relation of these gains and losses to the other variables such as original score, type of education in the period between the two test administrations, the occupation in 1961, job preferred when 21, youth organisation attended, newspapers read, books read and leisure activities.

Table 47 gives the overall picture of gains and losses for the group. The gains and losses in arithmetic and English have been grouped in intervals of five points of score in this and subsequent tables. Negative entries in the gains column represent losses.

On all three tests a small gain was made on average by the re-test group, but the changes were scattered over a wide band in each subject. The first question that arises is whether the

TABLE 48

MEAN GAINS IN TEST SCORES FOR DIFFERENT LEVELS OF 1960 SCORE

	Arithmetic		English			Composition	
1960 Score	Mean gain	No in group	Mean gain	No in group	1960 Score	Mean gain	No in group
80–89	−1·0	5					
70–79	0·9	32	1·7	3	8	−0·8	230
60–69	4·7	88	1·3	68	7	−0·6	422
50–59	3·3	259	2·5	278	6	0·1	96
40–49	2·4	394	2·6	439	5	0·3	486
30–39	0·7	447	2·2	437	4	0·7	85
20–29	0·0	308	1·8	327	3	1·0	301
10–19	−0·7	151	1·8	170	2	0·9	119
0– 9	0·9	54	4·0	29	0	2·0	2
	Not known	60	Not known	47		Not known	57
Totals	1·4	1798	2·3	1798	Totals	0·1	1798

gains were made mainly by the better pupils, ie, those scoring higher marks in the 1960 tests, or by the poorer pupils making up the leeway, or whether the gains were evenly spread over all levels of 1960 attainment. To clarify these points an analysis was made of the gains and losses for each level of the 1960 scores. The results are shown in table 48.

The pattern of gains shown in table 48 differs from test to test. In arithmetic, the gains are made largely by the pupils in the re-test group who scored *above* the average of 32 marks in the 1960 test. In English, all categories of level of score have gained and the gains are spread fairly evenly, the differences between them being statistically non-significant. In composition, however, the order of decreasing gains is almost exactly that of increasing level of 1960 score, those who scored high marks at the first test losing, and those who scored lower marks gaining. This is a good example of a phenomenon described as 'regression to the mean', to which reference must now be made.

The conclusion to be drawn then is that the 1798 young people re-tested increased their scores on average by small amounts. These gains were associated with above average 1960 scores in arithmetic, below average composition scores, but not with English scores.

REGRESSION TO THE MEAN

When a second test is given to a group of any size whose scores on a first test are known, the order of merit in the second test is unlikely to be the same as that on the first test. Those who were at the top of the first list will probably be some way down the second list, and those at the foot of the first list will probably be higher in the second. This is described as 'regression to the mean'. Their places at the top or bottom will be taken by others drawn from more central positions in the first list, and one group of candidates therefore moves *away from* the mean, but the generally accepted term 'regression to the mean' is taken to cover the whole situation.

The phenomenon occurs even where the second test is a repetition of the first test, as was the case in this inquiry. Tests are only imperfectly reliable; the less reliable they are, the more does regression to the mean show its effect.

The effects are that high scorers make lower scores in the second test and thus show losses at the second stage. Low scorers in the first test make higher scores at the second stage and thus show gains. It is therefore important that the size of the error be estimated.

It is possible to make corrections for the error, if the reliabilities of the tests are known. The corrected gains are known as the *true* gains to distinguish them from the *observed* gains. The correction is of a rather technical nature and details are therefore given in Appendix B. The results of the calculations are given in table 49.

It will be observed that the changes from observed gain to

TABLE 49

OBSERVED AND TRUE MEAN GAINS FOR DIFFERENT LEVELS OF 1960 SCORE

Arithmetic

1960 Score	0–9	10–19	20–29	30–39	40–49	50–59	60–69	70–79	80–89	Absent	Total
Mean observed gain	0·9	−0·7	0·0	0·7	2·4	3·3	4·7	0·9	−1·0		1·4
Mean true gain	−0·3	−1·9	−0·1	0·7	2·4	4·1	5·8	4·1	5·0		1·4
Number in category	54	151	308	447	394	259	88	32	5	60	1798

English

1960 Score	0–9	10–19	20–29	30–39	40–49	50–59	60–69	70–79	80–89	Absent	Total
Mean observed gain	4·0	1·8	1·8	2·2	2·6	2·5	1·3	1·7			2·3
Mean true gain	0·7	−0·5	2·3	2·4	2·6	2·7	4·4	3·3			2·3
Number in category	29	170	327	437	439	278	68	3		47	1798

Composition

1960 Score	0	1	2	3	4	5	6	7	8	Absent	Total
Mean observed gain	2·0	0·9	1·0	0·7	0·3	0·1	−0·6	−0·8			0·1
Mean true gain	1·0	0·2	0·4	0·6	0·2	0·3	−0·2	−0·3			0·1
Number in category	2	119	301	85	486	96	422	230		57	1798

true gain are mostly small and, when they are larger, the number of pupils involved is relatively small. As has been indicated, the effect shows to a maximum where the categories are those of 1960 score. For other classifications the effect will be less. For all of these reasons it was decided that the labour of converting observed gains to true gains would not be justified, and that observed gains would be used for the analyses which follow.

RELATION BETWEEN GAINS AND TYPE OF EDUCATION IN 1960–61

One question that arises is whether the gains are mainly attributable to the section of the group which continued in whole-time education and whether their gains did, in fact, counterbalance losses by those who had left whole-time education for employment. The analysis was carried still further, the eight categories of type of education described in chapter 7 being used. These were as follows:

Code No	Category
8	Those in senior secondary courses in 1960 and still at school in 1961
7	Those in junior secondary courses in 1960 and still at school in 1961
6	Those in full-time further education in 1960–61
5	Those attending day-release classes in 1960–61
4	Those attending part-time vocational classes in 1960–61
3	Those attending part-time non-vocational classes in 1960–61
2	Those not attending classes
X	No information available

The mean gains or losses for each of these categories are given in table 50.

The usual analysis showed that the differences in the mean gains for the various categories on each test were too large to be attributed to sampling. When the very small categories coded 3 and X were omitted from the further comparisons of pairs of means, the remaining categories fell into two distinct groups. The gains made by those in categories 8, 7 or 6 were significantly greater than were made by those in categories 5, 4 or 2. In both arithmetic and English a difference of three marks or more between the gains was statistically significant.

The analysis shows that the gains are, in fact, attributable mainly to the pupils who have continued their education on a whole-time basis at school or in further education. Those not attending classes have lost some at least of their skill in arithmetic,

TABLE 50

MEAN GAINS IN TEST SCORES CLASSIFIED BY TYPE OF EDUCATION 1960–61

	Arithmetic		English		Composition	
Type of education	Mean gain	No in category	Mean gain	No in category	Mean gain	No in category
8	5·8	559	4·3	569	0·2	563
7	4·9	109	5·2	108	0·7	108
6	2·5	156	4·7	155	0·5	157
5	0·5	130	0·9	133	−0·2	131
4	−1·6	334	0·7	336	−0·1	335
3	−2·5	22	0·9	22	0·1	22
2	−2·8	421	−0·4	420	−0·2	419
X	4·3	7	1·9	8	−0·3	6
Gain unknown		60		47		57
Averages and totals	1·4	1798	2·3	1798	0·1	1798

but the loss in English skills has been only slight. The ability to write a composition has improved slightly where pupils have continued at school or in full-time further education but has deteriorated only slightly in those leaving school.

RELATION BETWEEN GAINS AND OCCUPATION IN 1961

To some extent the classification by occupation in 1961 is a repetition of the classification of the preceding section, since those still at school and those in full-time further education in 1961, numbering over 800 and thus comprising nearly half of the 1961 group, remain in the categories of full-time education. The code used for this section was that described in chapter 7 (p 100). The mean gains for each category are shown in table 51.

The differences in mean gain for the various categories are too large to be attributed to sampling. Similar results were obtained for all three tests, categories falling into three main groups.

Group 1 Categories 0 and 1, ie, those still at school or in full-time further education

Group 2 Categories 7, 6, 4, 5, 3, 2, ie, those entering employment

Group 3 Categories 8, X, Y in which the numbers were too small to justify any conclusion.

The general picture, ignoring the very small categories, is that those members of the group who continued their education full-time made measurable gains in score on all three tests whereas those who left school and entered employment made losses or at best slight gains in score. There

TABLE 51

MEAN GAINS IN TEST SCORES CLASSIFIED BY OCCUPATION IN 1961

	Arithmetic		English		Composition	
Occupation in 1961	Mean gain	No of pupils	Mean gain	No of pupils	Mean gain	No of pupils
8 Professional	1·7	3	5·0	4	−0·3	4
7 Higher non-manual	−3·5	23	1·0	26	0·0	26
6 Lower non-manual	−1·3	224	0·9	219	0·2	219
5 Skilled manual	−0·9	268	0·1	269	−0·3	266
4 Semi-skilled manual	−2·3	246	−0·3	251	−0·2	248
3 Factory	−2·9	90	0·5	88	−0·4	91
2 Unskilled	−5·7	50	−0·4	50	−0·3	49
1 Full-time further education	2·5	156	4·7	155	0·5	157
0 School	5·7	668	4·5	677	0·4	671
X Not known	2·5	8	0·0	10	−1·1	8
Y Unemployed	2·5	2	5·0	2	0·0	2
Gain unknown		60		47		57
Averages and totals	1·4	1798	2·3	1798	0·1	1798

were slight variations from one test to another, eg, in the arithmetic test, category O (those still at school) gained significantly relative to category 1 (those in full-time further education), while category 2 (those in unskilled manual, agricultural or domestic jobs) lost significantly relative to categories 6 and 5.

It is interesting that the type of employment actually taken up by the young person bears little relationship to gains on the tests. Taken in conjunction with the previous comparison, based on type of education in 1961, the results underline even more strongly the relationship between educational instruction and gains in score.

RELATION BETWEEN GAINS AND OCCUPATION
PREFERRED AT AGE 21

In the questionnaire administered at the re-test stage there was an item 'What job would you like to have by the time you are 21?' The responses to this item were coded according to the scheme described in chapter 7 except that a category 'marriage' has been added for the benefit of 15 girls, and that the major and minor professions have been treated separately.

It seemed likely that those with ambitions for posts higher on the scale would have made greater gains than those with lower ambitions and the data were analysed from this point of view. The results are shown in table 52.

TABLE 52

MEAN GAINS IN TEST SCORES CLASSIFIED BY JOB PREFERRED AT 21

		Arithmetic		English		Composition	
Job preferred at 21		Mean gain	No in category	Mean gain	No in category	Mean gain	No in category
9	Major professional	4·8	192	4·1	195	0·2	195
8	Minor professional	3·0	146·	2·9	148	0·2	148
7	Higher non-manual	1·7	278	4·0	278	0·4	280
6	Other non-manual	−1·4	150	1·1	148	0·3	147
5	Skilled manual	−0·1	444	0·8	450	−0·1	446
4	Semi-skilled manual	−1·8	147	−0·2	152	−0·3	150
3	Factory	−2·9	29	2·3	28	−0·5	29
2	Unskilled	−2·7	13	−1·7	12	−0·1	13
0	Marriage	−1·1	14	0·3	15	−0·3	15
X	Unknown	3·9	325	3·5	325	0·2	318
	Gain unknown		60		47		57
	Totals		1798		1798		1798

The differences in mean gains for the various categories were too large to be attributable to sampling fluctuations. When the smaller categories were omitted, it was found that differences between gains amounting to three marks or more in arithmetic, or two marks or more in English, were statistically significant. None of the differences between gains in composition was significant.

The general picture which emerged was that on all three tests those members of the group who aspired to professional or higher non-manual employment made significantly higher gains than those who aspired to manual or unskilled jobs. There was a marked trend from gains by those who aspired to the major professions to losses by those who aimed only at unskilled work.

The number of 'no responses' was surprisingly large. It seems likely that pupils still at school either were uncertain of their ambitions or assumed that the question did not apply to them since it came under the general heading 'work' in the questionnaire.

In some ways the gains shown are to be expected, since the majority of those in the group who intended to enter the professions and the non-manual occupations remained at school and it has already been shown that those still at school made greater gains than those who had left.

RELATION BETWEEN GAINS AND NEWSPAPERS READ

One item in the questionnaire at the re-test stage was 'Which newspapers do you read regularly?' The coding scheme used for classifying the newspapers listed was given in chapter 7 (p 121). The gains in English and in composition for each of the categories are shown in table 53.

TABLE 53

MEAN GAINS IN TEST SCORES CLASSIFIED BY NEWSPAPERS READ

Newspapers read	English		Composition	
	Mean gain	No in category	Mean gain	No in category
8	3·3	199	0·1	197
7	2·2	1201	0·1	1193
6	1·8	174	0·3	176
5	1·0	39	−0·2	39
4	1·0	10	0·5	10
0	2·2	76	−0·3	78
X	2·6	52	0·8	48
Gain unknown		47		57
Totals		1798		1798

The differences in mean gain reach significance only at the 5 per cent level. In general, it would appear that the gains

made in test scores by the young person bore little relationship
to the type of newspaper read.

RELATION BETWEEN GAINS AND TYPE OF BOOK READ

The coding system used to classify the book last read by each
of the young people was given in chapter 7 (p 122).

Table 54 gives a summary of the mean gains for each category.
The differences among the means are too great to be attributed
to sampling.   The larger gains in all three tests were made by

TABLE 54

MEAN GAINS IN TEST SCORES CLASSIFIED BY BOOK READ

	Arithmetic		English		Composition	
Category of book read	*Mean gain*	*No in category*	*Mean gain*	*No in category*	*Mean gain*	*No in category*
7	4·1	130	3·6	132	0·5	132
6	4·0	178	4·2	183	0·2	179
5	1·6	374	1·7	383	0·0	377
4	1·4	289	2·5	289	0·2	287
3	0·3	72	2·5	71	−0·3	72
2	1·7	321	2·5	319	0·1	321
1	−2·8	23	−1·0	25	−0·9	24
0	−2·8	322	0·9	318	−0·1	322
X	4·8	29	3·5	31	1·3	27
Gain unknown		60		47		57
Totals		1798		1798		1798

those reading the more demanding books.   As has been pointed
out in chapter 7 these readers were, in the main, pupils continuing their education at school, a group already shown to have
made higher gains than the others made.   To some extent the
findings of this section are therefore a repetition of the earlier
findings.

RELATION BETWEEN GAINS AND MEMBERSHIP OF
YOUTH ORGANISATIONS

The classification system used has been described previously
in chapter 7 (p 119).   Table 55 gives a summary of the mean
gains for each category of classification.   Since some young
people belonged to more than one organisation the total

number (1877) exceeded the actual number of young people involved (1798). For this reason an analysis of variance was not carried out.

The results of the comparison were similar for both the English and arithmetic tests. Those young people who belonged to no

TABLE 55

MEAN GAINS IN TEST SCORES CLASSIFIED BY MEMBERSHIP OF YOUTH
ORGANISATION

		Arithmetic		English		Composition	
Category		Mean gain	No in category	Mean gain	No in category	Mean gain	No in category
8	Scouts or Guides	4·4	189	3·4	192	0·2	190
7	Boys' Brigade Girls'Guildry	2·4	133	2·5	134	0·0	132
6	Pre-service	3·0	46	2·7	46	0·0	46
5	Political	0·0	11	0·5	11	−0·5	11
4	Church clubs	2·2	214	3·6	218	0·4	220
3	Youth clubs (not Church clubs)	−0·1	205	1·6	208	0·0	205
2	Athletic clubs	2·2	56	1·9	57	0·5	56
1	Outdoor	3·0	25	4·0	25	0·1	24
0	None	0·6	892	1·9	892	0·0	892
X	Unknown	4·3	44	3·2	46	0·4	42

youth organisation, or belonged to youth clubs other than church ones, made lower gains than the other categories. Those who belonged to the Scouts and Guides tended to make above average gains; it has already been shown in chapter 7 that these organisations tended to find their membership among those continuing at school, so that their superiority may therefore be related to that fact.

RELATION BETWEEN GAINS AND TYPES OF LEISURE
ACTIVITY

The classification system used for leisure activities has been described previously in chapter 7 (pp 116-17). Table 56 gives a summary of the mean gains for each category of classification. As in the case of the youth organisations, many of the young people carried out more than one leisure activity and the total numbers in the categories do not tally with the number of young people for whom information was available (1798). For certain leisure activities, the number of young people participating was very small and these categories have been omitted from table 56. Those who indicated that dancing, the cinema and the variety theatre were their leisure activities made smaller gains than

TABLE 56

MEAN GAINS IN TEST SCORES FOR DIFFERENT LEISURE ACTIVITIES

		Arithmetic		English	
		Mean		*Mean*	
Activity		*gain*	*No*	*gain*	*No*
8	Music	1·5	200	3·3	205
6	Games and sports	2·1	1143	2·4	1151
5	Hobbies	1·5	443	2·5	447
4	Television	1·0	205	2·5	202
3	Cinema and variety				
	theatre	−0·4	320	1·8	318
2	Dancing	−0·3	399	1·6	398
0	Reading	2·4	571	3·4	576

the others, indeed on the arithmetic test they actually made losses, while those preferring reading and music made fairly large gains. These last are two types of activity followed much more by those still at school than by those in employment.

GAINS MADE BY UNDER AVERAGE PUPILS WHO
CONTINUED IN FULL-TIME EDUCATION

The Brunton Report[1] made it clear that 'the greatest need is to raise the level of attainment of the substantial number who are well below the present average'. It is therefore worth while to refine the figures of table 50 still further by extracting from the data the gains made by the under average pupils who continued with full-time education. These are given in table 57, in which figures for those who attended day-release classes have been included. For this table 'under average' has been interpreted as scoring under 30 in arithmetic or English or scoring C−, D or E in composition, in the 1960 tests. These border lines correspond to P44 in arithmetic, P43 in English and P40 in composition. The gains can be assessed from the changes in

[1] para 43.

percentile rank which is in each case based on the 1960 score distribution.

A correction for regression to the mean, to which reference was made on page 132, has not been applied to the figures in table 57, and the gains are therefore slightly overestimated.

TABLE 57

CHANGES IN PERCENTILE RANK AFTER A FURTHER PERIOD OF EDUCATION

	Arithmetic	*English*	*Composition*
(a) *At day school*			
1960 score and percentile	24·5 (P32)	23·9 (P30)	3·3 (P21)
1961 score and percentile	33·9 (P55)	30·9 (P46)	5·9 (P70)
Number in group	56	33	61
(b) *In full-time further education*			
1960 score and percentile	22·9 (P29)	23·1 (P27)	3·1 (P19)
1961 score and percentile	26·4 (P37)	29·5 (P43)	4·7 (P50)
Number in group	54	45	54
(c) *Day-release students*			
1960 score and percentile	18·3 (P20)	22·3 (P25)	2·9 (P17)
1961 score and percentile	19·5 (P21)	23·0 (P27)	3·5 (P25)
Number in group	51	62	49

It would appear from the figures that another year at school had the desired effect, but a year in full-time further education was not so efficacious and day-release had little effect. But it must be remembered that these pupils were not typical of all who left school at 15. A significantly higher proportion of them had parents in professional, non-manual or skilled occupations.

SUMMARY OF CHAPTER

Only 51 per cent of the original group were re-tested in 1961. Although it proved possible to re-test the great majority of the young people who remained at school or in full-time further education, the Committee was less successful in its attempts to contact those who entered employment, particularly so in the cases where the young persons did not attend classes at further education centres. For the latter group the response at the re-testing stage was as low as 24 per cent. Where the employers co-operated either by carrying out the testing on their own premises, or by releasing their employees for testing, the responses were also very good but it must be stated that only a minority of employers were willing to help.

Analysis of the scores showed that small gains were made on average by those re-tested on all three tests, but that there were wide variations in individual cases. Further investigation indicated that the re-test group could not be regarded as representative of the 1960 group since it contained a greater proportion of the 1960 high achievers and fewer from the lower levels of attainment. There was a definite association between level of attainment (as measured in 1960) and re-appearance for testing in 1961. Gains were associated with above average 1960 scores in arithmetic, with under average composition scores, but not with English scores. The gains were also related to the amount of education received in 1960–61 by the young person. Those who remained in full-time education made larger gains than those who attended part-time at further education centres, who in turn made greater gains than those who attended no classes at all. No relationship was found between gains in test score and type of employment taken up. It would appear that it is not the job, but whether the young person continues to receive any formal education, which determines whether he maintains his level of attainment or raises it.

The further comparisons made in the chapter served to reinforce the previous conclusion about the higher gains being made by those who remained in full-time education in 1961. Gains were found to be associated with job preference. There was a marked trend from gains by those who aspired to the major professions, to losses by those who aimed only at unskilled work. Those who read the more serious literature, eg the classics and modern novels, made higher gains than those who did not but in chapter 7 it was shown that those who intended to enter the professions remained at school in 1961 and that the reading of serious types of literature was confined mainly to those at school.

REPORTS BY STUDENT VISITORS

About a thousand members of the group were visited by students, and fifty-three of these students provided comments on their experiences. It must be stressed that these were subjective assessments written shortly after they had made the home visits and they did not know until after the visits that they would be called upon to give an account of them.

As has been indicated, the procedure was that a letter was sent to each of the young people inviting him or her to attend at a stated time and place and asking for co-operation in this matter. After that there was a reinforcing visit from a student. Students worked mainly in pairs and the majority of them were women.

Their observations were as follows:

1 They enjoyed this contact with homes and gained useful information about the background of pupils. They were mainly well received and invited into homes. In a few cases they gave sympathetic accounts of very poor living conditions under which pupils laboured.

2 Many of the ex-pupils had decided to ignore the letter for a variety of reasons:

> (*a*) A reaction against a return to school, classically stated in the opening quotation on the fly-leaf against chapter 1 of the Report *Half Our Future*. Typical examples were— 'The stuff we get at school is not needed in the factory', or 'I have never been any good at school'.
>
> (*b*) There was nothing in it for them.
>
> (*c*) Individuals were shy about attending a centre alone.
>
> (*d*) There was a fear that employers might find out about them.
>
> (*e*) There was general suspicion.

3 Parents, especially mothers, were much more interested than their children and usually promised to try to get the child to attend, but almost always stated that the decision would be left to the child.

4 The best single ploy for getting attendance was to mention that friends would be attending and to make arrangements to group people so that they could go together. Another useful method was to appeal to the responsibility of the ex-pupils and stress that they now had adult status. A few were flattered to have been asked to co-operate.

5 It was most exceptional to get a straight refusal. Pre-varication was common, such as 'I shall come if I have nothing else on'. Students forecast accurately whether an answer which could be interpreted as 'Perhaps' meant 'No'.

One straight refusal was because 'She's getting married, if you must know' from an angry mother. Another was on the grounds that the names of the letterhead of SCRE were unknown to the father and therefore of no account and not to be trusted!

6 Girls were much more willing to co-operate than boys.

7 Clearly a Friday night for testing, where this was the chosen night, was a bad choice, as many people had other engagements on that evening.

8 Some pupils attending further education classes had a long journey home from work and would have faced a further long journey out to a centre in the evening. This naturally damp-ened their enthusiasm. Such a situation only occurred in the scattered communities of the counties.

9 A common feature was the hunger of some parents for a person with whom to discuss educational matters and the future of their children. The students felt inadequate in giving such help as they did not know their own way through the jungle of further education regulations.

10 Several ex-pupils were contacted at their places of em-ployment. They did not like this as it made them feel 'kids' in the eyes of their workmates.

11 Although adequate notice of a date must be given, the actual testing session should follow very quickly after the contact visit, within three days if possible, as resolution fades quickly.

Without doubt, even fewer of those who had left school would have been available for the subsequent testings but for the personal visits, and the Council is greatly indebted to the students for their contribution.

Chapter 9

THE JUNIOR SECONDARY–SENIOR SECONDARY SYSTEM

INTRODUCTION

In chapter 6 it was shown that level of score in 1960 was associated with father's occupation, with rateable value of house, with type of secondary course (senior or junior secondary), and with job preferred when grown-up. It was associated with reason for leaving school in the sense that those wishing to

TABLE 58

PERCENTILES FOR SUB-GROUPS OF THE 1960 POPULATION

Variable	Sub-groups compared	Percentiles Arithmetic	English
Sex	Boys v Girls	50 v 50	46 v 56
Education area	1 v 2	53 v 42	
	5 v 2		57 v 47
Rateable value	Over £60 v unknown	73 v 44	
	Over £60 v under £19		73 v 43
Father's occupa-tion	Major profession v unemployed	82 v 37	84 v 34
Type of course	Sen Sec v Jun Sec	81 v 37	82 v 36
Reason for leaving (headmaster)	Not leaving v age, end of course	80 v 36	82 v 36
Reason for leaving (pupil)	Not leaving v wish to repay parents	78 v 36	79 v 34
Job preferred	Major profession v factory	84 v 26	
	Major profession v unskilled		88 v 24

remain at school had significantly higher scores than those who wished to leave, for whatever reason. The association with sex or with education authority area was slight.

The relative strengths of association of these variables with 1960 scores in arithmetic and English may be surmised from table 58 in which the mean scores are represented by the corresponding percentile ranks. The comparison is between the highest and the lowest scoring sub-group for each variable. Where the whole group is divided into eight or nine sub-groups, as occurs with the variables 'father's occupation' or 'reason for leaving', the comparison is between the two sub-groups at the extremes of the range and bigger differences seem likely than in the cases where there are only two sub-groups, eg, boys and girls. This must be borne in mind when the table is examined.

It is reasonable to suggest that 'reason for leaving' and 'job preferred when grown-up' should be regarded as consequences of, rather than causes of, school performance. When these two are eliminated from the discussion, the figures in table 58 suggest that the main factors associated with score in the tests were 'rateable value of house', 'father's occupation' and 'type of secondary education', with the last wielding the greater influence, since it produced percentile ranges of 44 and 46 in arithmetic and English from a simple dichotomy of the whole group.

This may be regarded as a 'blinding glimpse of the obvious', since the main purpose of allocation to different secondary courses was to provide suitable courses for the abler and the less able pupils. But the association which has been shown to exist between score and the other variables in the table makes it clear that the problem is not so simple and that other variables than ability were linked with allocation to secondary courses.

The present chapter contains a study of the relation between type of secondary course followed and the other variables. We look first at the 1960 data, secondly at the additional data obtained in 1961 from those who came forward for the second set of tests and questionnaires, then at the 1961 data for those who left school in 1960 to enter employment and finally at the 1960 data using the methods of discriminant analysis. Readers who wish to omit the sections which deal with this and other statistical methods will find these indented and can proceed to the remainder, which has been kept as free as possible of statistical terms.

Since most of the data are in the form of classifications by categories, the appropriate statistical test of association is usually the chi-square test. One refinement of this test is useful. Examination of the data or prior hypotheses may suggest the possibility of telescoping some of the categories of classification into larger but still homogeneous groups. A 'partitioned chi-square analysis'[1] makes it possible to verify that these larger groups can be regarded as homogeneous within themselves but differing significantly from each other. This enables us to decide where the significant differences lie.

While the chi-square technique indicates whether or not there is an association between two classifications, it does not measure the strength of the association. A useful measure for our purpose is the index of predictive association devised by Goodman and Kruskal,[2] which is based on the reduction of error in predicting one classification when the other is known. The coefficient (λ) ranges from 0, when the information about one classification is of no assistance in predicting the second, to 1, when the first classification enables the second to be made with complete certainty.

1960 DATA—RELATION BETWEEN SECONDARY COURSE AND FATHER'S OCCUPATION

The numbers of pupils in the two types of secondary course are shown in table 59, in which the technique of partitioned chi-square analysis has been used to reduce the number of separate categories. The association between secondary

TABLE 59

RELATION BETWEEN SECONDARY COURSE AND FATHER'S OCCUPATION

					Numbers in courses
Father's occupation	A Sen Sec	B Jun Sec	C Total	A as % of C	A as % of all Sen Sec
Professional or large employer	119	20	139	86	11
Small employer, self-employed or non-manual paid monthly	150	114	264	57	14
Non-manual paid weekly	161	200	361	45	15
Skilled manual, farmer	296	591	887	33	27
Father dead	66	205	271	25	6
Semi-skilled, unskilled, others	303	1322	1625	19	27
Totals	1095	2452	3547	31	100

[1] A E Maxwell, *Analysing Qualitative Data.* London: Methuen & Co, 1961, pp 52-56.
[2] L A Goodman and W H Kruskal, 'Measure of association for cross-classifications', *J Amer Stat Ass*, **49**, 1954, 732-46.

course and father's occupation was clearly established by this analysis.

There are two main conclusions to be drawn from this table. The first is that the chance of a pupil being allocated to a senior secondary course varied greatly between categories. The probability of the child of a professional man being so allocated was almost five times as great as that of the child of a father whose job was semi-skilled or unskilled.

The second is that the majority of the pupils in senior secondary courses in these areas came from homes where the fathers were in manual occupations. The apparent paradox arising from these two conclusions has been mentioned in chapter 6. It occurs because the large weight of numbers of pupils whose fathers were in manual occupations more than compensated for the smaller probability of a pupil in that category being allocated to a senior secondary course.

The value of λ in this case was 0·12; a knowledge of father's occupation reduces the probability of error in predicting type of secondary course by 12 per cent on the average.

1960 DATA—RELATION BETWEEN SECONDARY COURSE AND RATEABLE VALUE OF HOUSE

The figures in table 60 show that there was an association between these two variables. Apart from a curious inversion

TABLE 60

RELATION BETWEEN SECONDARY COURSE AND RATEABLE VALUE OF HOUSE

| | | | | | Numbers in courses |
Rateable value	A Sen Sec	B Jun Sec	C Total	A as % of C	A as % of all Sen Sec
Above £60	107	51	158	68	10
Between £40 and £59	375	563	938	40	34
Between £20 and £29	172	383	555	31	16
Between £30 and £39 and below £19	401	1348	1749	23	36
Unknown	40	107	147	27	4
Total	1095	2452	3547	31	100

at the £30 level, where pupils from houses rated between £20 and £29 had a higher chance of being in senior secondary courses than those from houses rated between £30 and £39, there was increased probability of being in a senior secondary course for those who lived in houses with higher rateable value. It is nevertheless true that more than half of the senior secondary pupils lived in houses with rateable values below £40.

A partitioned chi-square analysis showed that the association was significant and that the categories of rateable values could be combined to form four homogeneous groups. The value of λ was 0·05, ie, the rateable value was of low predictive power where the type of secondary course was concerned.

1960 DATA—RELATION BETWEEN SECONDARY COURSE AND SIZE OF FAMILY

Size of family has previously been found to be an important variable when progress in school has been studied. Macpherson[1] found that occupancy rate, which is closely related to size of family, had a high association with likelihood of completing a five-year course of secondary education, the chances varying from 4 in 5 for low occupancy rates to 1 in 10 for high occupancy rates.

Table 61 shows the numbers of pupils classified by size of family and secondary course, the family sizes having been

TABLE 61

RELATION BETWEEN SECONDARY COURSE AND SIZE OF FAMILY

| | | | | | Numbers in courses |
| | *A* | *B* | *C* | *A as %* | *A as % of all* |
Family size	*Sen Sec*	*Jun Sec*	*Total*	*of C*	*Sen Sec*
1 to 3	834	1301	2135	39	76
4	128	346	474	27	11
Over 4	106	755	861	12	10
Unknown	27	50	77	45	3
Total	1095	2452	3547	31	100

grouped into three categories after the usual analysis had shown that the association existed and that these three categories could be regarded as homogeneous. In particular, the differences in type of secondary course for children in family sizes 1, 2 and 3 were not significant.

---

[1] J S Macpherson, *Eleven-year-olds grow up*, Publication of the Scottish Council for Research in Education, 42. London: University of London Press Ltd, 1958.

These figures show that the pupil from a family containing fewer than four children had three times as great a chance of being in a senior secondary course as the child from a family containing more than four children.

Since families of one to three children predominated, the effect on the composition of the senior secondary course was not marked so far as these pupils were concerned, but the pupils from families with more than four children were under-represented to a marked degree. If there had been no association between size of family and type of secondary course we should have expected between 260 and 270 of them to be in the 1095 attending senior secondary courses; there were, in fact, only 106.

The value of λ was zero; knowledge of size of family was of no use in predicting the type of secondary course. This is because junior secondary pupils were in a majority in every size of family.

1960 DATA—RELATION BETWEEN SECONDARY COURSE AND JOB PREFERRED WHEN GROWN-UP

The usual analysis showed that there was an association between these two variables. There was little scope for combining groups, the only exceptions being the semi-skilled,

TABLE 62

RELATION BETWEEN SECONDARY COURSE AND JOB PREFERRED WHEN GROWN-UP

Job Preferred	A Sen Sec	B Jun Sec	C Total	A as % of C	Numbers in courses A as % of 1095	B as % of 2452
Major professional	321	32	353	91	29	1
Minor professional	164	110	274	60	15	4
Higher non-manual	176	215	391	45	16	9
Lower non-manual	105	236	341	31	9	10
Skilled manual	187	1016	1203	15	17	41
Semi-skilled manual, factory and unskilled	51	651	702	7	5	27
Unknown	91	192	283	32	8	8
Total	1095	2452	3547	31	100	100

factory and unskilled categories which could be taken as homogeneous for this purpose.

The association between secondary course and job preferred

is also reflected in the fall from 91 to 7 in the percentages shown in the fourth column of table 62.

This table also makes it clear that the senior secondary course must not be regarded mainly as a training ground for the professions, at least as far as the young people in this investigation were concerned. Less than half of the senior secondary pupils looked forward at the age of 15 to being members of professions when they had grown-up.

The value of λ in the prediction of job preference from course was only 0·07, showing a very small association between type of course and job preferred when grown-up. On the other hand λ was 0·34 when course was to be predicted from job preferred; a knowledge of the type of job preferred reduced by 34 per cent the probability of error in predicting the type of course followed.

THE 1961 SITUATION

As had been indicated in previous chapters, 1798 of the original group of 3547 came forward for the tests and questionnaires in 1961. Of those, 577 were still at school and in senior secondary courses, 237 had left school although in senior

TABLE 63

CHARACTERISTICS OF THE SIX 1961 GROUPS

| | | Percentiles in 1960 tests | |
Group	No	Arithmetic	English
Senior secondary			
at school, re-tested	577	85	87
left school, re-tested	237	74	72
not re-tested*	281	73	75
Junior secondary			
at school, re-tested	109	64	60
left school, re-tested	875	43	40
not re-tested*	1468	31	32
Total	3547		

* Of these a few were still attending school but were absent when the tests were given in 1961.

secondary courses, 109 were still at school following junior secondary courses and 875 had left school after following junior secondary courses. The percentile ratings corresponding to their average marks in the 1960 tests are shown in table 63, which also includes the percentile ratings for those who did not appear for the 1961 tests.

The rank order of the percentiles is clear. The group continuing to follow senior secondary courses at school had the highest percentile ranks in the 1960 tests. Their colleagues who had left school, although in senior secondary courses, had lower percentile ranks, but these were higher than those of the junior secondary group who had returned for a further year's schooling. This junior secondary group was above average for the whole 1960 group. The junior secondary pupils who had left school but took the 1961 tests were below the average for the whole 1960 group, but were in turn superior to the junior secondary group who did not appear for the 1961 tests.

1961 DATA—RELATION BETWEEN SECONDARY COURSE AND JOB PREFERRED WHEN 21

The members of the group who came forward for the tests and questionnaire in 1961 provided some additional data, of which use is made in the following sections. One question, to which reference has already been made in chapter 8, was what job the young person would like to have by the time he or she was 21. This is very similar to the question asked of the 1960 group and discussed in a previous section.

The usual analysis showed that there was once again an association between type of course and job preference. The value of λ had risen to 0·20, ie, knowledge of type of course reduced by 20 per cent the probability of error in predicting job preference. The figures are shown in table 64.

There were unfortunately many cases of 'no response' both from the senior secondary pupils still at school and from the junior secondary pupils who had left school. In the former case this probably arose from the faulty design of the questionnaire, where the question appeared under the general heading of 'work'.

A few girls (three in senior secondary courses and twelve who had left junior secondary schools) gave their job preference as 'marriage'. From the investigator's point of view these have unfortunately to be classified among the unknowns.

TABLE 64

NUMBERS AND PERCENTAGES OF YOUNG PEOPLE CLASSIFIED BY JOB PREFERENCE AND TYPE OF EDUCATION

Job preference	Senior Secondary		Junior Secondary		Total
	At school	Left school	At school	Left school	
Major professional	172 (30)	4 (2)	9 (8)	12 (1)	197 (11)
Minor professional	75 (13)	16 (7)	17 (16)	42 (5)	150 (8)
Non-manual	80 (14)	98 (41)	39 (36)	222 (25)	439 (24)
Manual	35 (6)	106 (45)	18 (16)	498 (57)	657 (37)
Unknown	215 (37)	13 (5)	26 (24)	101 (12)	355 (20)
Totals	577 (100)	237 (100)	109 (100)	875 (100)	1798 (100)
Percent of 1960 group	16	7	3	25	51

It is probably not advisable to draw conclusions from data which include so many 'no responses' but the figures suggest that about half of the senior secondary pupils still at school looked forward to being in professional posts by the age of 21, while those who had left school from senior secondary courses had ambitions evenly divided between non-manual and manual jobs. Most of the junior secondary pupils who had returned to school were hoping to have non-manual work of some kind at 21, but more than half of those who had left school from these courses hoped to be in manual occupations at that age.

1961 DATA—RELATION BETWEEN TYPE OF COURSE AND OCCUPATION IN 1961

The actual occupations of those who were tested in 1961 have been described in chapter 7. The usual analysis showed that there was an association between the type of secondary course and the type of occupation, and that it was possible to combine some of the categories into the larger homogeneous groups shown in table 65.

TABLE 65

TYPE OF COURSE AND OCCUPATION IN 1961

Numbers and percentages in, or formerly in

Occupation	A Sen Sec Courses		B Jun Sec Courses		C Total		A as % of C
School	577	(71)	109	(11)	686	(38)	84
Full-time further education	38	(5)	122	(12)	160	(9)	24
Professional and non-manual	82	(10)	175	(18)	257	(41)	32
Manual	105	(13)	430	(44)	535	(30)	20
Factory, unskilled	7	(1)	137	(14)	144	(8)	5
Unemployed or unknown	5	(1)	11	(1)	16	(1)	31
Totals	814	(100)	984	(100)	1798	(100)	

In predicting occupation from course the value of λ is 0·29, the second highest obtained in this set of calculations. This is largely due to the fact that the table includes the 577 senior secondary pupils who continued in their school courses. If they are excluded from the table, the association between type of course and occupation is still significant but the value of λ becomes zero. The most likely occupation in which to find either a senior secondary or a junior secondary former pupil who had entered employment was a manual one, either skilled or semi-skilled.

1961 DATA—RELATION BETWEEN SECONDARY COURSE AND LEISURE ACTIVITIES

One field in which there might be differences between the young people who had followed senior as contrasted with junior secondary courses is that of leisure activities. Information on this topic was obtained in the 1961 questionnaire. The first aspect considered is that of the number of activities, coded as in chapter 7. The usual analysis indicated that there was an association between type of course and number of activities but the value of λ was zero. The data are shown in table 66, in which the numbers have been grouped into four categories.

TABLE 66

SECONDARY COURSE AND NUMBER OF LEISURE ACTIVITIES

Numbers and percentages of young people

No of activities	Senior Secondary		Junior Secondary		Total
	At school	Left school	At school	Left school	
Many (4 or more)	199 (34)	63 (27)	37 (34)	127 (15)	426 (24)
Several (3)	158 (27)	77 (32)	30 (28)	236 (27)	501 (28)
Few (0–2)	215 (37)	93 (39)	37 (34)	499 (57)	844 (47)
Unknown	5 (1)	4 (1)	5 (5)	13 (1)	27 (1)
Totals	577 (100)	237 (100)	109 (100)	875 (100)	1798 (100)

These figures show that the senior secondary pupils and the junior secondary pupils still at school had on the average a greater number of leisure activities than did those junior secondary pupils who had left school. It is, however, possible that the figures reflect the greater willingness of the first three groups to give detailed responses to the question 'What do you do in your spare time?'

The reader may be more interested in the nature of leisure time activities than in their quantity and some estimate of this may be obtained from table 67, in which the leisure activities listed by the young people have been classified in accordance with the following code.

Code	Description of activity
9	Youth leadership or voluntary service to others
8	Music
7	Theatre
6	Games and sports
5	Hobbies
4	Television
3	Pictures, radio, variety theatre
2	Dancing
1	Visiting cafes, going out with friends
0	Reading
X	Membership of youth organisations

Since many listed more than one activity the total number in any column exceeds the number of young people in the group; the percentages are based on the number in the group.

TABLE 67

SECONDARY COURSE AND LEISURE ACTIVITY

Numbers listing various activities and percentages in each group listing them

Leisure activity	Senior Secondary				Junior Secondary					
	At school		Left school		At school		Left school		Totals	
9	15	(3)	5	(2)	7	(6)	9	(1)	36	(2)
8	97	(17)	32	(14)	9	(8)	73	(8)	211	(12)
7	10	(2)	3	(1)	1	(1)	5	(1)	19	(1)
6	424	(73)	168	(71)	72	(66)	511	(58)	1175	(65)
5	165	(29)	62	(26)	35	(32)	195	(22)	457	(25)
4	61	(11)	28	(12)	16	(15)	105	(12)	210	(12)
3	72	(12)	41	(17)	15	(14)	201	(23)	329	(18)
2	89	(15)	62	(26)	12	(11)	249	(28)	412	(23)
1	22	(4)	8	(3)	0	(—)	31	(4)	61	(3)
0	281	(49)	71	(30)	55	(50)	182	(21)	589	(33)
X	316	(55)	134	(57)	69	(63)	360	(41)	879	(49)
Total no of activities	1552		614		291		1921		4378	
Number in group	577	(100)	237	(100)	109	(100)	875	(100)	1798	(100)

In all types of course, games and sports were the most popular type of activity and there was little difference in this respect between the senior secondary and the junior secondary pupils. Membership of youth organisations (which included youth clubs) was also popular in all groups; more will be said about this type of activity in a later section. The main differences among the group were in music, where the senior secondary pupils showed more interest, in reading, where pupils still at school showed greater interest, and in dancing, in which the young people who had left school were much more interested than those still at school. One interesting feature of the table is the close correspondence of the percentages for the two groups still at school.

1961 DATA—RELATION BETWEEN SECONDARY COURSE
AND TYPE OF READING

In chapter 7 it was pointed out that the major differences in reading habits lay between those of the group who continued at school and those who entered employment. It was therefore not surprising to find the same tendency in the figures for the four sub-groups of the previous sections. For the analysis the categories of books listed on p 122 in chapter 7 were

TABLE 68

SECONDARY COURSE AND TYPE OF BOOK LAST READ

Numbers and percentages of young people

| | Senior Secondary | | Junior Secondary | | |
Type of book	At school	Left school	At school	Left school	Total
7, 6	209 (36)	39 (16)	32 (29)	39 (4)	319 (18)
5, 4, 3, X	228 (40)	121 (51)	53 (49)	388 (44)	790 (44)
2	111 (19)	50 (21)	20 (19)	172 (20)	353 (20)
0	29 (5)	27 (11)	4 (4)	276 (32)	336 (19)
Totals	577 (100)	237 (100)	109 (100)	875 (100)	1798 (100)

grouped into three sets; those in the category of literature coded 7 and 6; those coded 5, 4, 3 and X, ie, more ephemeral books and the few which were unclassifiable; and the response 'none' which was coded 2. For these classifications the value of λ was zero; knowledge of type of course was of no help in predicting type of book read since for all courses the most popular choice was in categories 5, 4, 3 or X. The numbers and percentages for the grouped categories are shown in table 68.

It will be observed that the junior secondary pupils who had returned to school were very similar in reading habits to the senior secondary pupils still at school. The senior secondary pupils who had left school occupied an intermediate position between their colleagues still at school and the junior secondary pupils who had left school.

1961 DATA—RELATION BETWEEN SECONDARY COURSE AND USE MADE OF LIBRARIES

The question 'Do you borrow books from the library?' was asked in the 1961 questionnaire. The responses from those who had left school are shown in table 69.

TABLE 69

TYPE OF COURSE AND USE OF LIBRARIES

Numbers and percentages of young people formerly in

	Senior Secondary course		Junior Secondary course		Total	
Using libraries	119	(50)	311	(36)	430	(39)
Not using libraries	101	(43)	448	(51)	549	(49)
No response	17	(7)	116	(13)	133	(12)
Totals	237	(100)	875	(100)	1112	(100)

There is a significant association between type of course and use made of libraries. Those who have followed senior secondary courses made greater use of the library system. On the other hand the differences in the percentages were not great, and the value of λ was only 0·04, when use of library was predicted from type of course.

1961 DATA—RELATION BETWEEN SECONDARY COURSE AND YOUTH ORGANISATION

The coding used for youth organisations was given in chapter 7 page 119, where it was pointed out that some young people were members of several organisations. As this complicates both the tabulation and the analysis (the chi-square and the λ calculations not being applicable where an individual is included in more than one category of a distribution), resort was made to the principle of a hierarchy of code numbers, any young person included under code 8 being excluded from code 7, and so on.

The hierarchy could be regarded as one of tightness of organisation.

As some of the frequencies were rather small, the smaller categories were combined to form the following larger groups: (*a*) uniformed organisations (codes 8, 7 and 6); (*b*) church clubs (code 4); (*c*) youth clubs other than church clubs (code 3); (*d*) athletic and outdoor clubs (codes 2 and 1); (*e*) unclassified (codes 5 and X); and (*f*) none (code 0). These provided the data in table 70.

TABLE 70

SECONDARY COURSE AND MEMBERSHIP OF YOUTH ORGANISATIONS

Numbers and percentages of young people

Youth	*Senior Secondary*		*Junior Secondary*		
Organisation	*At school*	*Left school*	*At school*	*Left school*	*Total*
Uniformed	160 (28)	63 (27)	31 (29)	119 (14)	373 (21)
Church club	75 (13)	27 (11)	17 (16)	79 (9)	198 (11)
Youth club	33 (6)	29 (12)	9 (8)	118 (13)	189 (10)
Outdoor	16 (3)	8 (3)	5 (3)	26 (3)	55 (3)
Unclassified	32 (6)	7 (3)	7 (6)	18 (2)	64 (4)
None	261 (45)	103 (43)	40 (37)	515 (59)	919 (51)
Totals	577 (100)	237 (100)	109 (100)	875 (100)	1798 (100)

The usual analysis showed that there was an association between type of course and type of youth organisation. The junior secondary pupils who had left school were more likely than the others to be found in no organisation, and were much less likely to be found in a uniformed organisation. The value of λ was zero, ie, knowledge of type of course was of no assistance in predicting the type of youth organisation a young person was likely to favour.

1961 DATA—RELATION BETWEEN SECONDARY COURSE
AND MOTHER AT WORK

There has been discussion among educationalists for some time on the effects on a child of the mother going out to work. In the 1961 questionnaire the young person was asked whether the mother worked outside the home. The replies were coded to provide the data in table 71, in which 'working' is to be interpreted as in a paid post outside the home. Widows were included in the working and not-working categories.

The usual analysis revealed a significant association between type of course and whether the mother was working. The senior secondary pupils who remained at school had less than the average share of working mothers, while the junior secondary pupils who had left school had more than the average share of working mothers. The pupils who had left school from senior

TABLE 71

SECONDARY COURSE AND MOTHER'S OCCUPATION

Mother's status	Senior Secondary		Junior Secondary		
	At school	Left school	At school	Left school	Total
Working regularly	124 (21)	68 (29)	31 (29)	318 (36)	541 (30)
Not working regularly	449 (78)	164 (69)	73 (67)	545 (62)	1231 (68)
Others	4 (1)	5 (2)	5 (5)	12 (1)	26 (1)
Totals	577 (100)	237 (100)	109 (100)	875 (100)	1798 (100)

Numbers and percentages of young people

secondary courses and those following junior secondary courses who had returned to school had the same percentage of working mothers, each being about the average for the whole group.

The coefficient λ was zero, ie, knowledge of whether the mother was working was of no assistance in predicting type of secondary course. This is so because a majority of the mothers in each of the four categories did not work outside the home. The overall proportion of working mothers was 30 per cent.

1960 DATA—RELATION BETWEEN TYPE OF COURSE AND GROUPS OF VARIABLES

Although type of course has been shown to be only weakly associated with father's occupation, rateable value of house or size of family when these were taken singly, it may be that the association would be found to be stronger if these three were taken together. The appropriate statistical technique for a problem of this kind is discriminant analysis. In this method the variables are combined in a linear fashion to form a discriminant function. The weights given to the variables in the function are fixed so that the difference between the means of the functions for the senior secondary and the junior secondary groups is the greatest possible multiple of the standard deviation within each group.

The method was applied first to the groups defined as senior secondary and junior secondary by the schools in 1960. There were 1095 pupils in the first group and 2452 in the second, but complete data were available for only 878 in the first group and 1894 in the second. The analysis (details of which are given in Appendix D) showed that the appropriate discriminant for each pupil was obtained approximately by adding twice the code number for father's occupation to 1·1 times the code number for rateable value and subtracting 2·2 times the code number for size of family. In terms of these units the distance between the means of the senior and junior secondary pupils was 3·6, which was large enough to be statistically significant at the 0·1 per cent level. In other words, the senior secondary and junior secondary *groups* of pupils differed to a recognisable extent in terms of their background of father's occupation, type of house and size of family when all three were taken together with appropriate weights.

But the overlap of the two distributions was substantial. The standard deviation of each was 3·6, so that the point midway between the two means was only half a standard deviation above the mean of the junior secondary distribution and the same distance below the mean of the senior secondary distribution. Figure 9, in which overlap A represents the senior secondary pupils in the junior secondary area, and overlap B represents the junior secondary pupils in the senior secondary area, illustrates the position for these variables. If the broken line passing through the point midway between the means is taken as the line of demarcation between the distributions then 31 per cent of the junior secondary group fell into the senior secondary area and 31 per cent of the senior secondary group into the junior secondary area. This percentage is termed the probability of mis-classification. If we were given the father's occupation, rateable value of house, and size of family for a pupil and classified him by the use of the discriminant function based on these variables we should be wrong, ie, disagree with the original allocation, in 31 per cent of the decisions. It is also true to say that we should be correct in 69 per cent.   If we allocated the pupils at random to the 878 senior secondary and 1894 junior secondary places we should be wrong in 44 per cent of the decisions.   We therefore conclude that father's occupation, rateable value of house and size of family, taken together, were far from being decisive determinants of type of secondary course.

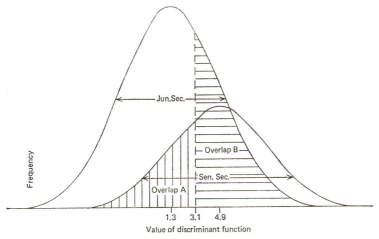

FIGURE 9   Distributions of discriminant functions constructed from father's occupation, rateable value of house and size of family

There was a rather different picture when a fourth variable, ie, job preferred when grown-up, was brought into the discriminant function.   The distance between the means widened to 9·9 and the standard deviation increased to 6·0.   The difference between the means was again statistically significant at the 0·1 per cent level and the overlap had been greatly reduced.   The probability of mis-classification was reduced to 20 per cent. But it may be argued that 'job preferred' was for many pupils a consequence of the type of course followed.   The pupil in the senior secondary course realised that he was in the stream leading to university or college and to the professions; the pupil in the junior secondary course realised that accesss to the professions was becoming more and more difficult as the years went by and set his sights accordingly.   The difference between the overlap of 31 per cent found for the three variables and the overlap of 20 per cent found when 'job preferred' was added to the three may be taken as a measure of the extent to which selection for secondary education gave further rigidity to the classification into two different groups of young people.

It has already been shown that 'job preferred' was closely related to scores in the arithmetic and English tests used in the inquiry. This suggests that we might use as classifying variables the scores in the tests. The mean scores of the senior secondary groups in the 1960 tests were 45·4 in arithmetic and 45·6 in English. The corresponding scores for the junior secondary group were 26·5 and 26·7. If the demarcation lines between higher and lower scores are taken to pass midway between these means, so that pupils scoring 0 to 35 in arithmetic or from 0 to 36 in English are classified as 'lower scorers' and those with higher marks as 'higher scorers', then the probability of misclassification into senior secondary and junior secondary groups on this basis would be 20 per cent. Thus the overlap in scores in the tests was equal in size to the overlap in the discriminant functions constructed from father's occupation, rateable value of house, size of family and job preferred when grown-up.

There is still a further way of examining the data. We know that of the 1095 pupils in senior secondary courses in 1960, only 577 returned to school and were available for testing in 1961. With the wisdom that follows the event we might describe these as senior secondary 'stayers'. Similarly, if we exclude from the original group of 2452 junior secondary pupils the 109 who returned to school and took the 1961 tests, we have 2343 junior secondary leavers. How do these groups differ in sociological background?

Of the 577 and 2343 only 506 and 1949 yielded the full data required for the discriminant analysis. Using father's occupation, rateable value, and family size as the three variables, the function produced a difference of 8·0 between the means of the two groups, which was highly significant statistically and a standard deviation of 3·7. The line of demarcation passed through the point which was 0·7 times the standard deviation distant from each of the means, ie, the probability of mis-classification was 24 per cent. Thus the change of definition and of groups under consideration reduced the probability of mis-classification from 31 per cent to 24 per cent.

Introduction of the fourth variable—job preferred—once again altered the position, and on this occasion to a marked degree. The difference between the means of the two groups rose to 35·6, which was highly significant; although the standard deviation within groups rose to 12·5, the increase was not as great as that of the distance between the means, and the line of demarcation passed through the point which was 1·4 times the standard deviation away from each mean. This corresponds to an 8 per cent probability of mis-classification. An examination of the discriminant function shows that the greater accuracy of classification was very largely due to the presence of the fourth variable, ie, job preferred when grown-up.

The discriminant functions which had been obtained from these re-defined groups were then used to classify the pupils who had either (a) left from senior secondary courses before 1961, or (b) returned to school although in junior secondary courses in 1960. In some cases the sociological data were insufficient to enable a classification to be made. When the three-variable function was used the results were as follows.

TABLE 72

CLASSIFICATION OF PUPILS USING THREE SOCIOLOGICAL VARIABLES

Numbers classified as

Course	Junior Secondary leavers	Senior Secondary stayers	Unclassified	Total
Senior secondary	282	181	55	518
Junior secondary	59	35	15	109
Totals	341	216	70	627

It will be observed that the majority of those who left senior secondary courses at the earliest opportunity had the same characteristics as those of the junior secondary leavers. On the other hand, only a minority of those from junior secondary courses who returned to school had the same characteristics as those of the senior secondary stayers.

For the four-variable[1] function the numbers were as shown in table 73.

TABLE 73

CLASSIFICATION OF PUPILS USING FOUR SOCIOLOGICAL VARIABLES

Numbers classified as

Course	Junior Secondary leavers	Senior Secondary stayers	Unclassified	Total
Senior secondary	280	183	55	518
Junior secondary	50	45	14	109
Totals	330	228	69	627

[1] Father's occupation, rateable value of house, size of family, job preferred when grown-up.

The addition of the fourth variable did not substantially change the position as compared with that indicated in table 72.

In pointing out the association that existed between these sociological variables and the likelihood of schooling being continued after the compulsion to attend was gone, the writers of this report do not suggest that these variables should have been used at the transfer stage to make allocation procedures more 'efficient'. The point of view they prefer to take is that knowledge of the sociological variables and of their association with school progress should enable authorities, teachers and others to give the additional support which the figures have shown to be desirable where the pupil's environment is not favourable to scholastic success.

The main conclusion of this section is that the factors of father's occupation, rateable value of house, and size of family, when they were combined in the most efficient way, could distinguish those following senior secondary courses from those following junior secondary courses in about two-thirds of the cases. The variable which could add most strength to the discriminating power of the battery was 'job preferred', which was already known to be strongly linked to the scores in the arithmetic and English tests and hence to the attainments of the pupils.

SUMMARY OF CHAPTER

At the time of the investigation, pupils entering secondary courses in Scotland were allocated either to senior secondary courses leading to the award of a school leaving certificate or to junior secondary courses of a less academic character. The association which the inquiry showed to exist between type of secondary course and other variables such as father's occupation, test performance, and job preference led to a study of the relation between the type of course followed and these variables taken singly or in combination.

The analysis described in this chapter shows that the main single difference between the two groups was in their attainments in the basic skills, the senior secondary group being markedly superior on average, but even in these there was a considerable overlap. The senior secondary group was drawn from a wide range of social backgrounds, the majority coming from homes where the father was in a manual occupation. Their leisure interests tended to be more intellectually demanding than those of the young people who had followed junior secondary courses but again the overlap was considerable. The predominating leisure time interest of both groups was games and sport. About 70 per cent of the senior secondary group looked forward at the age of 15 to holding posts in the professions or in non-manual occupations when they grew up, while the corresponding proportion for the junior secondary group was about 25 per cent.

When the variables of father's occupation, rateable value of house, size of family and job preferred were combined in such a way as to give the maximum discrimination between the two groups, the overlap between the groups was still about 20 per cent. The overlap could be reduced to 8 per cent if all four variables were used and two new groups were defined. The first, defined as the 'senior secondary stayers', included only the 577 pupils who continued in senior secondary courses after school-leaving age; the second, defined as the 'junior secondary leavers', included only the 2343 who left school from junior secondary courses at the earliest opportunity.

While the data showed that sociological variables did not completely determine type of secondary education, they did reveal the handicaps which face the pupil from the large family who has a parent in an unskilled manual occupation. If children in these circumstances are to make the most of their talents, the school and society must be prepared to give particular attention to compensatory provision for their individual needs.

Chapter 10

COMMENTS AND SUMMARY

COMMENTS

The investigation reported in the preceding chapters arose partly from the comments of employers on the attainments of young people entering industry. The Brunton Report[1] suggested that in any consideration of these matters account should be taken of the loss of learning which takes place when study is discontinued by young people for even a relatively short period. While this may be important where more complicated skills are concerned or a good deal of memory work is involved, the evidence provided in chapter 8 of this report suggests that loss of learning cannot be regarded as an important factor where the basic skills of arithmetic and English are concerned. The losses after ten months' absence from any kind of formal education appear to have been relatively slight.

The evidence in chapter 8 can only suggest, but not establish, this conclusion. That part of the investigation suffered from the reluctance of the Scottish adolescent to undergo examination in a school situation once he or she had left school. It is not possible to draw definite conclusions from a 51 per cent response rate, especially where the 51 per cent is known to be unrepresentative of the total population. On the other hand, there were enough representatives of the under-represented sections to suggest trends.

In so far as the attainments of the young people who left school at 15 were concerned a great deal of information is given in chapter 5 on the attainments not only of the young person of average ability of that age in 1960 but also of those at several different levels of ability.

The reason most frequently given by the pupils for leaving school at the age of 15 was that they preferred work to school. On the other hand, the reason most frequently given by teachers

[1] *From School to Further Education.*

was that the pupil had reached 'school-leaving age' or had completed the appropriate course. The adult world at that time seems to have accepted 'school-leaving age' to mean the age when a boy or girl is expected to leave school unless there is a strong argument for not doing so.

The evidence of chapter 7 underlines what is generally known—that most of the pupils with higher attainments continued at school after the 'school-leaving age' and were not available at that age for industry. There were still some bright young people who left school for employment as soon as they were free to do so, but it is generally accepted that their numbers were small compared to those of the 1920s and the 1930s. Figure 8 (page 103) and Appendix E, tables 92 and 93, show the position in 1961; two-thirds of the young people in the top fifth of the attainment range were in attendance at school or in full-time education. The same diagram and tables make it clear that there was room for improvement in the selection procedures for entry to different types of occupation.

Of those who returned to school for a further year or entered full-time further education there was a small number whose attainments in 1960 had been well below the average. The year at school had the effect of bringing the average of this group up to the average obtained by all pupils in 1960. It should be noted that these young people were relatively few in number and not representative of the whole population.

Under the system of secondary education operating in Scotland in 1960, pupils were allocated at the age of 12 either to senior secondary courses leading to the award of a national certificate[1] (Ordinary grade after four years, Higher grade after five years), or to junior secondary courses lasting normally for three years but not leading to the award of a national certificate. The system was not so rigid as has sometimes been stated, and some pupils gained O grade, and a small number passed H grade, after spending most of their secondary years in junior secondary courses, but there was nevertheless a fairly clear-cut distinction in most schools between pupils following courses leading to presentation for a certificate, and those in non-certificate courses. From the data provided in the investigation

---

[1] At that time the Scottish Leaving Certificate.

it was possible to compare the two groups in a number of ways. It was found that the main differences between them were of two kinds, those of attainments in the tests of arithmetic and English, and of job preference. Sociological variables such as father's occupation, rateable value of house occupied, and size of family also distinguished the two groups to some extent. In their leisure interests and activities they had much in common.

Since 1961 there have been significant changes in day school education in Scotland. There has been a considerable development of comprehensive secondary schools, and school systems were changing to this new basis as the report was being written. In some schools, common courses were being developed at the early stages of secondary education. There is also evidence[1] that standards of achievement are rising in Scottish primary schools and this will have a consequential effect on standards in the secondary schools.

Whether any or all of these changes, or others yet to be introduced, have had the effect of raising the basic attainments of the average and the less able young people is a question for further investigation at an appropriate time. The data provided in the present report may contribute to the provision of a suitable base-line for comparison.

SHORT SUMMARY

1 The group of young people taking part in the inquiry was defined as those attending education authority schools in five areas of Scotland and attaining the age of 15 in the summer term, 1960. They numbered 3547.

2 They were given tests of basic skills in arithmetic and English, wrote a composition, and supplied information about themselves. This information was supplemented by the school.

3 After an interval of ten months, 51 per cent of the group attempted the same tests, wrote a second composition and supplied further information. The remaining 49 per cent were unable or unwilling to attend for the tests.

[1] *Rising Standards in Scottish Primary Schools: 1953–63*, Publication of the Scottish Council for Research in Education, 56. London: University of London Press Ltd, 1968.

4 The tests are given in full in the report, along with a detailed analysis of the performance of the young people. The main correlates of high scores were type of secondary course (senior or junior secondary) and job preferred when grown-up.

5 The commonest reason given by pupils for leaving school was 'I prefer work to school', while the majority of teachers gave 'age' or 'end of course' as the reason.

6 Those who continued at school for a further year were mostly, though not entirely, those who had made higher than average scores in the 1960 tests. The children of professional and self-employed men tended to continue at school; those of the semi-skilled and unskilled workers tended to leave at the first opportunity.

7 Those who left school entered a wide range of occupations; almost half of the girls entered non-manual occupations and almost half of the boys took up skilled manual work. There was a strong association between level of attainment in the 1960 tests and type of occupation chosen. Nevertheless the test scores of the entrants to skilled and semi-skilled manual work were scattered over a wide range.

8 The young people who took some form of further education after leaving school were mainly those who had made higher scores in the tests.

9 The great majority of those who undertook part-time further education did so in evening rather than in day-release classes.

10 The overwhelming majority of the whole group pursued leisure activities, usually of two or three different types; games and sports, reading, hobbies, and dancing were the most popular. Less than half belonged to a youth organisation or club.

11 The reading of literature was restricted almost entirely to those who remained at school. Over one-third of those who had left appeared to have read little of any description, other than the newspapers, since they had left school.

12 The group which came forward for the re-testing in 1961 was not representative of the whole 1960 group, those who had left school and undertaken no further education being thinly represented. Those who did come forward showed, on average, slight gains in score on the tests.

13 In the year 1960, the organisation of secondary education was based on a system of allocating pupils at the age of 12 to senior secondary courses extending over five or six years and leading to presentation for the Scottish Leaving Certificate, or to junior secondary courses lasting for three or four years which had no national terminal certificate. The data collected in this investigation showed that children of parents in professional and non-manual occupations had higher probability of entering senior secondary courses, but that these courses had a preponderance of young people whose fathers were in manual occupations. The main difference between the senior secondary and junior secondary groups was in their attainments in the basic skills measured by the tests and in their job preferences, most of the former group looking forward at the age of 15 to holding posts in the professions or in non-manual occupations, while the main preference of the latter group was for manual work.

14 A further year at school was sufficient to bring the attainments of those pupils who had made less than average score in 1960 up to the average level attained by their colleagues at the age of 15.

15 Whether the standards reached in the basic skills of English and arithmetic by the young people were adequate for the demands of the 1960s is a problem to which this investigation does not provide the answer. Nor was it intended to. What it does provide is a fairly detailed picture of these attainments along with related socio-economic information about the young people with whom this survey was concerned.

Appendix A

THE ASSESSMENT OF THE COMPOSITIONS

The method adopted in the assessment of the compositions was suggested by Mr D McMahon, a member of the Committee. It consisted essentially of two parts, the first being the preparation of templates to serve as standards for the assessment of the compositions, and the second the use of these templates.

The first stage of the method required the selection of a random sample of 100 essays from the group. The Committee's first decision was to select 100 compositions from the 5263 available from the 1960 and 1961 tests. This involved the selection of 69 from the 3467 produced at the 1960 tests.

The data available for stratification of the sample were sex and education area of the pupil. It was not possible to make use of type of course as details were not known in most cases. The basic table was therefore as follows.

NUMBERS OF PUPILS PROVIDING COMPOSITIONS

Area	1	2	3	4	5
Boys	635	182	104	673	183
Girls	587	183	96	643	181

From this table there was prepared a cumulative frequency table 635, 635 + 587 = 1222, 1222 + 182 = 1404 . . . 3286 + 181 = 3467. The selection of 69 from the total of 3467 gave a selection ratio of 1 in 50. A randomly chosen starting point of 20 in the first group of 635 gave the number to be selected from that group as 13, these being numbers 20, 70, 120, . . . 620 *if the compositions were in random order*. Similarly, numbers 670, 720, . . . 1220 in the second group of 587 would be selected, giving 12 from that group. On this basis the number of compositions to be drawn from each group was calculated.

The actual selection of compositions within each group was

randomised by the use of a table of random sampling numbers. Thus in the first group the numbers of the compositions to be selected were taken from the table as 616, 609, 159, 387, 79, 380, 70, 631, 432, 309, 32, 572, 607. No numbers were actually entered on the compositions; the investigator counted down the pile to number 32, withdrew that composition, counted on to number 70 and so on.

At a later date the Committee decided to select the 100 compositions entirely from the 1960 group. The process described above was therefore repeated to obtain a further 31 compositions from the 1960 group. The 100 selected essays were arranged in alphabetical order, and three nominal rolls were prepared (also in alphabetical order). Three judges were used to assess the standards of the 100 selected essays working independently of each other and using impression marking only. The first judge arranged the essays in order of merit and put down the position in order of merit beside each name on his roll. He then sorted the essays back into alphabetical order retaining his own list, and passed them on to a second judge who repeated the procedure and passed the essays to a third judge who again carried out the ranking of the essays in order of merit. The three judges, having each marked the essays independently, were brought together and a general discussion took place on discrepancies in each other's list. To estimate the initial agreement among the three judges, correlation coefficients were calculated for each pair of judges. The values obtained were $r_{12} = 0.895$, $r_{13} = 0.824$, $r_{23} = 0.787$. The multiple correlation between the ratings of the first judge and the best weighted combination of ratings of the other two was $R_{1.23} = 0.916$. These values are very satisfactory, showing a considerable measure of agreement among the three judges, the first of whom was a senior lecturer in applied psychology with experience of this type of grading, the second a lecturer in English in a college of education, and the third a relatively inexperienced assistant lecturer in applied psychology. As a result of this discussion the three judges produced an agreed order of merit list. The actual essays at the following points in the agreed list were extracted: the 5th from the top, the 20th, the 50th, the 80th, and the 95th from the top. The five essays were labelled

A, B, C, D, E respectively and became the templates used in the assessment of all the compositions.

Reproductions of the five essays can be found on pages 79 to 81.

For the second stage of assessment, twenty-five secondary school teachers were invited to form a marking team. A meeting was held in Moray House College of Education at which the method of assessment to be used was explained to the markers. Each marker was given a set of templates and a number of essays to be assessed. He read through his batch of essays and allocated them to one of the five grades A to E according to how closely they corresponded to one of the templates. For a large number of essays the distribution of the gradings should be approximately 10, 20, 40, 20, 10 per cent for A to E respectively. The actual distribution obtained for all the markers was 8, 19, 39, 22, 12 per cent which is very satisfactory and indicates that the method of assessment had achieved its purpose.

Appendix B

REGRESSION TO THE MEAN

It has already been pointed out that the tables of gains or losses of score for each level of initial score give some indication that regression to the mean is an important factor. This is particularly striking in the case of the composition test where the order of decreasing gain is almost exactly that of increasing initial score.

EXTRACT FROM TABLE 48

1960 score	0	2	3	4	5	6	7	8
Gain in score	2·0	0·9	1·0	0·7	0·3	0·1	−0·6	−0·8

If the two tests were perfectly reliable, these would be the best estimates we could make of the pupil's gains and losses. But when errors of measurement enter, making the tests only imperfectly reliable, the observed gain is not generally equal to the true gain, ie, the gain from which any bias due to errors of measurement has been removed as far as that is possible.

This problem has been carefully examined by Frederic M Lord[1] who has devised formulae for estimating true gain. This is defined as the difference between true score on initial and final tests, assumed to be parallel forms. In our case these parallel forms are identical tests. Subject to certain assumptions about normality of distributions and linearity of regression, Lord has shown that the true gain $\hat{G}$ is given by

$$\hat{G} = \bar{G} + a(x - \bar{x}) + b(y - \bar{y})$$

where $\bar{G}$ is the mean gain of the whole population, x and $\bar{x}$ are scores and mean scores in the first test, y and $\bar{y}$ refer to the second test and a and b are coefficients involving the reliabilities of the tests, their variances and their inter-correlation. Complete formulae are given at the end of this note.

---

[1] Frederic M Lord, *Elementary Models for Measuring Change*. Research Memorandum of the Educational Testing Service, Princeton, NJ, 1962.

To obtain reliability coefficients for the 1960 tests, 100 scripts were chosen at random from those of the pupils taking both the 1960 and 1961 tests. Answers pattern were prepared and from these figures and the variances of the total scores the Kuder Richardson coefficient of reliability was calculated. The values were for arithmetic 0·946 and for English 0·939. Strictly speaking, these are coefficients of internal consistency rather than coefficients of equivalence but the two types of coefficients are closely related, and the second one was not obtainable from the data. The total data are shown in table 74.

TABLE 74

MATERIAL FOR CALCULATING TRUE GAINS

	Arithmetic	English
Reliability of 1960 test	0·946	0·939
Reliability of 1961 test	0·963	0·951
Correlation between tests	0·895	0·896
$\dfrac{\text{Variance of 1961 test}}{\text{Variance of 1960 test}}$	1·20	1·12

The equation for estimating true gain in arithmetic can then be written

$$\hat{G} = 0·613y - 0·529x - 2·66$$

which can be written

$$\hat{G} = 0·613(y - x) + 0·084x - 2·66$$

showing that the true gain is about half of the observed gain $(y - x)$ with a small adjustment for initial score and another for the mean gain of the whole group.

Examples of the changes are shown below.

1960 score	1961 score	Observed gain	True gain
5	15	10	4
35	55	20	13
35	15	−20	−12
85	85	0	4

Table 75 can now be transformed into table 76, a table of *true* gains and losses. Both tables are given for comparison.

Two effects of the changes will be observed. The first is that the range of gains and losses has been considerably reduced at all levels of initial score and in the total. The second is that

TABLE 75

DISTRIBUTION OF GAINS AND LOSSES IN ARITHMETIC FOR DIFFERENT LEVELS OF 1960 ARITHMETIC SCORE

Gain in score	1960 score									X	Total
	0–9	10–19	20–29	30–39	40–49	50–59	60–69	70–79	80–89		
18 to 22			3	7	1	7	3				21
13 to 17		2	15	24	33	23	11	1			109
8 to 12	5	6	31	47	73	56	16	3			237
3 to 7	8	27	62	107	98	54	25	9	2		392
− 2 to + 2	33	58	76	121	86	58	20	8	2		462
− 7 to − 3	8	49	70	69	62	37	7	10			312
− 12 to − 8		9	41	49	29	17	5	1			151
− 17 to − 13			8	21	8	7	1		1		46
− 22 to − 18			2	2	4						8
X		5	8	8	7	4	1			27	60
Total number	54	156	316	455	401	263	89	32	5	27	1798
Mean gain	0·9	−0·7	0·0	0·7	2·4	3·3	4·7	0·9	−1·0		1·4

TABLE 76

DISTRIBUTION OF TRUE GAINS AND LOSSES IN ARITHMETIC FOR DIFFERENT LEVELS OF 1960 ARITHMETIC SCORE

Gain in score	1960 score									X	Total
	0–9	10–19	20–29	30–39	40–49	50–59	60–69	70–79	80–89		
13 to 17				7	1	7	3	1			19
8 to 12		2	18	24	33	79	27	3	2		188
3 to 7	5	6	93	154	171	54	45	17	2		547
− 2 to + 2	41	85	76	121	148	95	7	11	1		584
− 7 to − 3	8	49	111	118	29	24	6				346
− 12 to − 8		9	8	23	12						52
− 17 to − 13			2								2
X		5	8	8	7	4	1			27	60
Total number	54	156	316	455	401	263	89	32	5	27	1798
Mean gain	−0·3	−1·9	−0·1	0·7	2·4	4·1	5·8	4·1	5·0		1·5

little change has been made in the mean gain at each level of 1960 score, except for the small numbers in the 70 to 79 and 80 to 89 group where the true gain is much larger than the observed gain.

A similar position holds for the gains and losses in English, as shown in tables 77 and 78. The equation is

$$\hat{G} = 0.503y - 0.442x - 1.16$$

or

$$\hat{G} = 0.503\,(y - x) + 0.061 - 1.16.$$

These tables provide similar conclusions to those drawn from the arithmetic tables. The range of true gains is much less than the range of observed gains, but the mean gain at each level is little changed except for the small groups at either end of the distribution.

It is difficult to make similar calculations for the composition test, because the reliability of this test cannot be derived by the method used for the arithmetic and English tests. There is a further complication in that, to the unreliability of the pupil, we must add the unreliability of the examiner, the test of composition not being an objective test with a standard answer key.

We know that the inter-correlation between the two administrations was 0.60 and the ratio of the standard deviations 1.1. The mean score in 1960 was 5.3 and in 1961 it was 5.4. If we assume a reliability coefficient of 0.80 we find that the equation for the true gain is

$$\hat{G} = 0.58(y - x) + 0.07x - 0.33$$

an equation very similar to those for arithmetic and English.

The mean gains calculated for the different levels of 1960 score on these assumptions are shown in table 79.

TABLE 77

DISTRIBUTION OF GAINS AND LOSSES IN ENGLISH FOR DIFFERENT LEVELS OF 1960 ENGLISH SCORE

Gain in score	1960 score								X	Total
	0–9	10–19	20–29	30–39	40–49	50–59	60–69	70–79		
23 to 27	1									1
18 to 22			3	1	2					6
13 to 17	2	3	14	22	13	2				56
8 to 12	4	17	36	68	80	30	4			239
3 to 7	8	56	98	122	136	118	24	2		564
− 2 to + 2	10	60	94	131	118	89	28	1		530
− 7 to − 3	4	29	66	68	69	36	10			283
− 12 to − 8		5	10	20	21	2	2			60
− 17 to − 13		1	6	5	4	1				12
X			1	7	4	3			31	47
Total number	29	171	328	444	443	281	68	3	31	1798
Mean gain	4·0	1·8	1·8	2·2	2·6	2·5	1·3	0·7		2·3

TABLE 78

DISTRIBUTION OF TRUE GAINS AND LOSSES IN ENGLISH FOR DIFFERENT LEVELS OF 1960 ENGLISH SCORE

Gain in score	1960 score								X	Total
	0–9	10–19	20–29	30–39	40–49	50–59	60–69	70–79		
8 to 12	1		17	23	15	2	4			62
3 to 7	6	20	134	190	216	148	52	2		768
− 2 to + 2	18	116	160	199	187	125	12	1		818
− 7 to − 3	4	34	16	25	21	3				103
X		1	1	7	4	3			31	47
Total number	29	171	328	444	443	281	68	3	31	1798
Mean gain	0·7	−0·5	2·3	2·4	2·6	2·7	4·4	3·3		2·3

TABLE 79

DISTRIBUTION OF GAINS AND LOSSES IN COMPOSITION FOR DIFFERENT LEVELS
OF 1960 COMPOSITION SCORE

	1960 score									
	0	2	3	4	5	6	7	8	X	Total
Number	2	121	303	85	492	97	425	232	41	1798
Mean observed gain	2·0	0·9	1·0	0·7	0·3	0·1	−0·6	−0·8		0·1
Mean true gain	1·0	0·2	0·4	0·6	0·2	0·3	−0·2	−0·3		0·1

Lord's formula for true gain

The true gain $\hat{G}$ of a pupil scoring x in the first test and y in the second test, is given by the formula

$$\hat{G} = \bar{G} + b_{Gx.y}(x - \bar{x}) + b_{Gy.x}(y - \bar{y})$$

where $\bar{G}$ = mean observed gain made by all pupils

$\bar{x}$ = mean score of all pupils in first test

$\bar{y}$ = mean score of all pupils in second test

and $b_{Gx.y}$ and $b_{Gy.x}$ are coefficients depending on the reliabilities, variances and inter-correlations of the two tests.

If $\quad\quad r_{xx}$ = reliability of the first test

r_{yy} = reliability of the second test

S_x = standard deviation of first test

S_y = standard deviation of second test

r_{xy} = correlation between the two tests

then $\quad\quad b_{Gx.y} = \dfrac{(1 - r_{yy})r_{xy}S_y/S_x - r_{xx} + r^2_{xy}}{1 - r^2_{xy}}$

$b_{Gy.x} = \dfrac{r_{yy} - r^2_{xy} - (1 - r_{xx})\, S_x r_{xy}/S_y}{1 - r^2_{xy}}$

Appendix C

STAYING ON AT SCHOOL

Of the 1798 young people who were re-tested in 1961, 686 were still at school and 577 of these were following a course of study leading to the Scottish Certificate of Education examinations which many of them sat in 1962. The Research Council, as part of another project (Assessment for Higher Education), has been following up the careers of the 11,000 young people in Scotland who were presented in at least one subject on the Higher grade for the first time in the 1962 Scottish Certificate of Education examinations, and it has been possible to obtain further information about the later educational progress of those young people who appear in both projects. In the final analysis 445 (12·5 per cent) of the original group of 3547 were found to be part of the later project.

Tables 80 and 81 show the distribution of these 445 students by sex, in terms of their 1960 scores in arithmetic and English respectively, and for purposes of comparison show the corresponding distribution of the whole group tested in 1960. The numbers from each score-range entering some form of full-time higher education are also given. In the tables, higher education has been divided into three categories (1) University (2) College of Education or (3) Central Institution.

Approximately equal numbers of boys and girls were presented for SCE examinations in 1962 or subsequent years. Of those presented, 86 boys and 106 girls were found to have entered some form of higher education at a later date. This total of 192 entrants to higher education represents 5·4 per cent of the original group and 43 per cent of those presented for the Scottish Certificate of Education in 1962 from the group.

Although more girls than boys entered higher education the type of education undertaken was very different. Almost half of the girls entered colleges of education to take a three-year

TABLE 80

NUMBERS IN GROUP, NUMBERS PRESENTED FOR SCE EXAMINATIONS AND NUMBERS ENTERING HIGHER EDUCATION RELATED TO ARITHMETIC SCORE IN 1960

Arithmetic score in 1960	Boys No in group	Boys No presented for SCE	Boys Type of HE Univ	Boys Type of HE CI	Girls No in group	Girls No presented for SCE	Girls Univ	Girls Type of HE C of E	Girls CI
85–89	2	2	2		1	1			
80–84	4	3	1						
75–79	9	8	4		5	5	3	4	
70–74	13	11	4	1	9	5	7		
65–69	26	14	5	3	16	11	5	1	1
60–64	42	24	9	3	27	14	4	2	4
55–59	62	33	9	2	57	25	7	8	6
50–54	104	33	11	7	97	40	2	9	3
45–49	146	31	3	1	118	33	4	6	5
40–44	168	26	4	5	186	36		9	1
35–39	205	18	2		204	21	1	6	2
30–34	222	8	1	1	226	15		3	
25–29	199	5	1	1	207	6		2	
20–24	179	5		2	189	3			
15–19	134				129	1			
<15	279				200				
Absent	42				40				
Totals	1836	221	60	26	1711	216	33	50	22

TABLE 81

NUMBERS IN GROUP, NUMBERS PRESENTED FOR SCE EXAMINATIONS AND NUMBERS ENTERING HIGHER EDUCATION RELATED TO ENGLISH SCORE IN 1960

English score in 1960	Boys				Girls				
	No in group	No presented for SCE	Type of HE Univ	CI	No in group	No presented for SCE	Univ	Type of HE C of E	CI
70–76	1	1	1		2	7	5	1	3
65–69	6	6	4		9	33	11	9	5
60–64	25	18	6	3	41	48	9	15	6
55–59	66	47	16	3	75	52	7	16	7
50–54	89	45	17	6	116	45	1	7	2
45–49	119	41	6	6	158	25		2	
40–44	183	34	8	2	223	9			
35–39	215	22	2	4	231	2			
30–34	211	8		2	223				
25–29	233	1			195				
20–24	251				165				
15–19	190	1			135				
<15	227				103				
Absent	20				35				
Totals	1836	224	60	26	1711	221	33	50	23

course of training for primary school teaching. Thirty-one per cent of the girls entered a degree course at a university while the remainder (22 per cent) enrolled at one of the central institutions. On the other hand, 70 per cent of the boys entered universities while the remainder were attending a central institution.

A feature of tables 80 and 81 is the number of pupils of relatively low attainment (as measured in 1960) who were successfully presented for the Scottish Certificate of Education and subsequently entered higher education. This is particularly evident in the case of arithmetic where of five boys who scored 24 (P31) or less in 1960, three entered higher education. To show this more clearly the data of tables 80 and 81 have been presented in a slightly different way in tables 82 and 83 by combining the various categories of score into four larger groupings. The boundaries chosen for these larger groupings were the 88th (87th for arithmetic scores), 68th, and 42nd percentile levels. The reasons for choosing these particular cutting points were (a) just over 12 per cent of the group were presented for the Scottish Certificate of Education examinations, therefore a division at or near this point (the 88th percentile level) will show how many of the pupils in the group with high attainments were presented, (b) just over 31 per cent of the group were allocated originally to senior secondary courses on transfer from primary school and a division at or near this point (the 68th percentile level) will show how many pupils below this level of attainment (as measured in 1960 after 3 years' secondary schooling) were presented for the Scottish Certificate of Education examinations, (c) only two pupils (both boys) from below the 42nd percentile level of attainment in English in 1960 were presented for the Scottish Certificate of Education examination and this level was therefore selected as a lower limit for the third category.

In chapter 6 the superiority of the girls over the boys in the 1960 English tests was mentioned. This superiority is shown again in table 83 where there are many more girls of high attainment than boys and a correspondingly large excess of boys of relatively low attainment in the 1960 group.

The position has changed considerably, however, when one

TABLE 82

NUMBERS IN GROUP, NUMBERS PRESENTED FOR SCE EXAMINATIONS AND NUMBERS ENTERING HIGHER EDUCATION RELATED TO PERCENTILE LEVEL OF ATTAINMENT IN ARITHMETIC IN 1960

| | Boys | | | | Girls | | | | |
| | No in group | No presented for SCE | No entering Higher Educ Univ | CI | No in group | No presented for SCE | No entering Higher Educ Univ | CE | CI |
Percentile level of 1960 Arithmetic score									
Above 87th percentile	262	128	38	16	212	101	26	24	5
68th–87th percentile	314	57	14	6	304	69	6	15	9
42nd–68th percentile	427	26	6	1	430	36	1	9	6
Below 42nd percentile	791	10	2	3	725	10		2	2

TABLE 83

NUMBERS IN GROUP, NUMBERS PRESENTED FOR SCE EXAMINATIONS AND NUMBERS ENTERING HIGHER EDUCATION RELATED TO PERCENTILE LEVEL OF ATTAINMENT IN ENGLISH IN 1960

| | Boys | | | | Girls | | | | |
| | No in group | No presented for SCE | No entering Higher Educ Univ | CI | No in group | No presented for SCE | No entering Higher Educ Univ | CE | CI |
Percentile level of 1960 English score									
Above 88th percentile	187	117	44	12	243	140	32	41	14
68th–88th percentile	302	75	14	8	381	70	1	9	9
42nd–68th percentile	426	30	2	6	454	11			
Below 42nd percentile	901	2			598				

considers presentations for the Scottish Certificate of Education examinations. At every level of attainment the proportion of boys remaining at school to be presented for the SCE examinations was higher than that of the girls so that most, if not all, of the previous sex differences in distribution of attainment had disappeared. However, many more boys than girls of low attainment in English reached this stage of schooling (14 per cent of the boys compared with 5 per cent of the girls). The figures in table 83 show that 40 per cent of the very able boys and girls (above 88th percentile level) had left school without being presented for the Scottish Certificate of Education examination, while the corresponding figures for those in the next category of attainments (the 68th–88th percentile levels) was 79 per cent. There was therefore a considerable drain of young talent away from the academic system of education at all levels of attainment, even the highest.

The tendency for girls to choose colleges of education for higher education has been mentioned previously. It is remarkable that those girls who did embark on a university education came with only one exception from the highest level of attainment (ie, the top 12 per cent of the population), whereas the boys who enrolled at university had a much broader spectrum of attainment.

Many of the conclusions drawn with reference to the data of table 83 apply equally to table 82. However, the spread of achievement in arithmetic was much wider than for English both for those presented for the Scottish Certificate of Education examination and for those who proceeded to higher education. Fifty-two per cent of the boys and girls with very high attainments in arithmetic had left school without being presented for the Scottish Certificate of Education compared with the 40 per cent of the students with very high attainments in English. On the other hand, there were considerable numbers of boys and girls with relatively low levels of attainment in arithmetic who stayed on at school, sat the Scottish Certificate of Education examination and proceeded to higher education. No significant differences between the sexes as regards arithmetical achievement was found.

It would appear that a low level of attainment in arithmetic is not necessarily a barrier to success in higher education since only one of the sixteen lowest scorers in arithmetic who entered higher education has so far withdrawn from his course. These sixteen students all came from below the 56th percentile level of the 1960 group. The same is not true of attainment in English. No one from below the 42nd percentile level entered higher education and of the eight in table 83 who were in the 42nd–68th percentile range, four have already failed or withdrawn from their courses.

Since the report on the project 'Assessment for Higher Education' will deal extensively with the factors affecting success in higher education on a much wider sample it is not appropriate to carry out any further analysis of the data relating to the group involved in this present project.

In summary it can be said that just over 12 per cent of the group were presented for the Scottish Certificate of Education examination and just over 5 per cent proceeded to some form of higher education. For girls, university education was restricted almost exclusively to those with a very high level of attainments, the majority of girls preferring to enter a college of education to train for primary school teaching. A large majority of the boys preferred to enter university and it was drawn from a much wider spectrum of achievement than the girls. Many of the very able boys and girls originally in the top 12 per cent of the group in terms of attainment left school without being presented for the Scottish Certificate of Education examinations and this represents a very serious loss of talent from the academic system. For those who did enter higher education there was some evidence that a low level of attainment in arithmetic was not a severe obstacle to success but that an above average attainment in English was essential to success.

Appendix D

DISCRIMINANT ANALYSIS

In chapter 9 (pp 161–7), reference was made to the use of discriminant analysis in attempting to classify secondary school pupils as senior or junior secondary on the basis of sociological variables only. The description of the procedure followed was necessarily brief and a fuller treatment of the analysis is given here.

The data used in the first analysis were restricted to size of family (X), father's occupation (Y), and rateable value of home (Z). These variables had been categorised previously on the basis of the responses made by the group of pupils in 1960.

The first step in the analysis was to apply the 'partitioned chi-square' technique (cf p 148) to assess the homogeneity or otherwise of the various categories. As a result of this test it was possible to telescope some of the categories and those actually used in the analysis are shown below.

Size of family	X	
1–3 children	1	
4 children	2	
More than 4 children	3	

Father's occupation	Initial Y	Amended Y
Professional or large employer	5	6
Small employer, self-employed or non-manual paid monthly	4	4
Non-manual paid weekly	3	3
Skilled manual or farmer	2	2
Semi-skilled, unskilled and others	1	1

Rateable value of house	Initial Z	Amended Z
Above £60	4	5
£40–£59	3	3
£30–£39	2	2
£20–£29	1	1
£0–£19		

To carry out the statistical analysis it is necessary to assume that for each variable the categories can be regarded as having

189

a natural order and that there is therefore a continuous variable underlying them. On this basis it is possible to assign to each category a numerical value. Initially therefore the variables were quantified, father's occupation having scores from 5 to 1, rateable value scores 4 to 1 and size of family scores 1 to 3.

A check was then made on the linearity of the regression of each variable on type of secondary course. To carry out the regression analysis senior secondary course was scored 1 and junior secondary course 0.

The results of this analysis indicated that while the variable 'size of family' did not depart significantly from a linear regression with 'type of secondary course' this was not true of 'father's occupation' or 'rateable value'. Since linearity of regression is one of the basic assumptions inherent in applying the discriminant analysis technique it was decided to re-score 'father's occupation' giving the category 'professional or large employer' a score of 6 in place of 5. Similarly, 'rateable value' was re-scored giving the category 'Above £60' a new value of 5 in place of 4. The remaining categories of all variables retained their original values. These changes made the regressions linear.

The aim of the discriminant analysis is to find that linear function of the three variables which will maximise the ratio of the difference between the means of the two groups to the standard deviation within groups.

The linear function is then of the form

$$a = aX + bY + cZ$$

The values of a, b, and c are found by solving the equations

$$a\Sigma x^2 + b\Sigma xy + c\Sigma xz = d_x$$
$$a\Sigma xy + b\Sigma y^2 + c\Sigma yz = d_y$$
$$a\Sigma xz + b\Sigma yz + c\Sigma z^2 = d_z$$

where x, y, and z are deviations from the means of X, Y and Z respectively and d_z, d_y, d_z are the differences in mean score between the senior secondary and junior secondary groups on each variable.

When the data shown in table 84 were used in these equations, the values of a, b and c, each multiplied by the same constant 10^4, were found to be

$$a = -2\cdot233$$
$$b = +2\cdot019$$
$$c = +1\cdot100$$

and the linear function was

$$\alpha = -2\cdot233X + 2\cdot019\,Y + 1\cdot100\,Z$$

The average values of α for the senior secondary and junior secondary groups were $4\cdot8734$ and $1\cdot2890$ respectively, and the distance between the means was $3\cdot5844$. The borderline, midway between the means, was at $3\cdot0812$.

TABLE 84

DATA FOR DISCRIMINANT ANALYSIS

	Senior Secondary group		Junior Secondary group	
N	878		1894	
ΣX	1144		3372	
$\bar{X}$		1·3030		1·7804
ΣY	2302		3149	
$\bar{Y}$		2·6219		1·6626
ΣZ	1987		3285	
$\bar{Z}$		2·2631		1·7344
ΣX^2	1838		7524	
ΣY^2	8168		6937	
ΣZ^2	5859		7489	
ΣXY	2923		5343	
ΣXZ	2575		5956	
ΣYZ	5867		5804	

$$d_x = -0\cdot4774$$
$$d_y = 0\cdot9593$$
$$d_z = 0\cdot5287$$

A F test was then applied to check that the discriminant function α does indeed discriminate significantly between the two groups. Table 85 summarises the results of this test for the data.

The value of F is highly significant, ie, the set of α values is not homogeneous and the discriminant function could be used to discriminate between the two groups.

From the data it is also possible to calculate the probability of mis-classification of an individual whose group is uncertain

when the discriminant function is used to allocate him to either
the senior secondary or junior secondary group. The variance
within groups is shown in table 85 to be 12·949, corresponding
to a standard deviation of 3·598. The borderline between the
groups is therefore at a distance 3·5844/2×3·598, ie, 0·498
units of standard deviation from either mean. The corresponding area of the tail of the normal curve is 0·31 and this is
the probability of mis-classification.

TABLE 85

ANALYSIS OF VARIANCE OF α BETWEEN AND
WITHIN SECONDARY GROUPS

Source of variation	Degree of freedom	Sum of squares	Mean square	F	Probability
Between groups	3	7707	2569·2	198·4	P < 0·001
Within groups	2768	35844	12·949		
Totals	2771	43551			

Similar analyses were carried out for the four variable cases
and also for the cases where 'senior secondary' and 'junior
secondary' were defined in a more restricted fashion.

Appendix E

TABLE 86

SCORES IN ARITHMETIC TEST 1960

Frequencies of total scores by area, sex and type of course

	Area					Sex		Course		
Score	1	2	3	4	5	Boys	Girls	SS	JS	Total
90–95										
85–89				3		2	1	3		3
80–84	2			2		4		3	1	4
75–79	4	2	1	4	3	9	5	14		14
70–74	9	2		9	2	13	9	19	3	22
65–69	10	5	1	23	3	26	16	39	3	42
60–64	17	7	3	35	7	42	27	59	10	69
55–59	38	5	13	54	9	62	57	97	22	119
50–54	80	9	7	84	21	104	97	157	44	201
45–49	87	25	9	127	16	146	118	146	118	264
40–44	131	28	18	137	40	168	186	193	161	354
35–39	155	31	33	147	43	205	204	149	260	409
30–34	189	45	31	145	38	222	226	87	361	448
25–29	158	50	30	133	35	199	207	55	351	406
20–24	123	45	22	127	51	179	189	36	332	368
15–19	82	36	17	97	51	134	129	9	254	263
10–14	60	27	12	96	44	132	107	4	235	239
5–9	49	21	7	87	18	109	73		182	182
0–4	16	15	2	20	5	38	20		58	58
Absent	23	17		37	5	42	40	25	57	82
Totals	1233	370	206	1367	371	1836	1711	1095	2452	3547
Mean	33·06	28·93	32·08	33·22	30·36	32·40	32·36	45·41	26·50	32·35

TABLE 87

SCORES IN ENGLISH TEST 1960

Frequencies of total scores by area, sex and type of course

	Area					Sex		Course		
Score	1	2	3	4	5	Boys	Girls	SS	JS	Total
70–74	1				2	1	2	3		3
65–69	3		2	7	3	6	9	15		15
60–64	16	4	4	33	9	25	41	62	4	66
55–59	45	18	5	55	18	66	75	132	9	141
50–54	66	19	9	81	30	89	116	180	25	205
45–49	93	34	15	93	42	119	159	197	80	277
40–44	145	33	28	150	50	183	223	204	202	406
35–39	171	49	24	160	42	215	231	161	285	446
30–34	179	39	30	150	36	211	223	88	346	434
25–29	158	41	29	170	30	233	195	30	398	428
20–24	147	45	21	159	44	251	165	17	399	416
15–19	110	44	18	124	29	190	135	1	324	325
10–14	50	23	8	89	17	119	68		187	187
5–9	32	17	7	57	9	92	30		122	122
0–4	6	2	1	9	3	16	5		21	21
Absent	11	2	5	30	7	20	35	5	50	55
Totals	1233	370	206	1367	371	1836	1711	1095	2452	3547
Mean	32·7	31·3	32·6	32·1	35·2	30·6	34·8	45·6	26·7	32·6

TABLE 88

SCORES IN COMPOSITION TEST 1960

Frequencies of scores by sex and type of course

	Sex		Course		
Score	Boys	Girls	SS	JS	Total
8	125	163	252	36	288
7	266	378	373	271	644
6	80	111	56	135	191
5	443	497	270	670	940
4	120	89	34	175	209
3	441	328	88	681	769
2	291	117	8	400	408
0	7			7	7
X	63	28	14	77	91
Totals	1836	1711	1095	2452	3547
Mean	4·5	5·2	6·2	4·2	4·8

TABLE 89

PERCENTILES FOR 1960 SCORES IN ARITHMETIC AND ENGLISH

Arithmetic				English			
Mark	*P*	*Mark*	*P*	*Mark*	*P*	*Mark*	*P*
75 and over	100	32	50	65 and over	100	31	47
69–74	99	31	47	62–64	99	30	44
65–68	98	30	45	60–61	98	29	42
62–64	97	29	43	58–59	97	28	39
60–61	96	28	40	57	96	27	37
58–59	95	27	38	56	95	26	34
57	94	26	36	55	94	25	32
55–56	93	25	33	54	93	24	30
54	92	24	31	53	92	23	27
53	90	23	29	52	91	22	24
52	89	22	27	51	90	21	22
51	88	21	25	50	88	20	20
50	87	20	23	49	87	19	18
49	86	19	21	48	86	18	16
48	84	18	19	47	84	17	14
47	83	17	18	46	83	16	12
46	82	16	16	45	81	15	10
45	80	15	15	44	79	14	9
44	78	14	13	43	77	13	8
43	76	13	12	42	74	12	7
42	74	12	11	41	72	11	6
41	72	11	9	40	70	10	5
40	70	10	8	39	67	9	4
39	67	9	6	38	64	8	3
38	65	8	5	37	61	7	2
37	62	7	4	36	59	4–6	1
36	60	6	3	35	57	0–3	0
35	58	5	2	34	54		
34	55	3–4	1	33	52		
33	53	0–2	0	32	49		

TABLE 90

ANSWER PATTERNS OF ARITHMETIC TEST
(106 BOYS AND 99 GIRLS)

Section 1

Item	Correct B	Correct G	Wrong B	Wrong G	Not attempted B	Not attempted G
1	98	97	8	2	0	0
2	97	93	9	6	0	0
3	81	79	23	20	2	0
4	86	87	15	12	5	0
5	51	60	41	30	14	9
6	76	76	28	23	2	0
7	94	91	7	7	5	1
8	64	71	31	27	11	1
9	65	71	37	28	4	0
10	66	74	26	22	14	3
11	73	78	26	18	7	3
12	51	54	45	43	10	2
13	54	60	26	33	26	6
14	45	55	33	35	28	9
15	64	71	16	21	26	7
16	39	49	40	40	27	10
17	58	76	15	10	33	13
18	56	74	17	10	33	15
19	37	40	24	28	45	31
20	42	39	36	45	28	15
21	52	62	21	16	33	21
22	50	54	23	24	33	21
23	32	38	23	31	51	30
24	21	20	20	26	65	53
25	13	15	18	22	75	62
26	38	45	17	19	51	35
27	16	14	19	16	71	69
28	33	31	5	5	68	63
29	8	3	15	19	83	77
30	29	33	4	14	73	52
31	17	19	17	22	72	58
32	14	13	13	10	79	76
33	12	13	12	13	82	73
34	10	9	7	6	89	84
35	9	10	7	8	90	81
36	1	1	5	3	100	95
37	2	5	5	3	99	91
38	1	1	2	5	103	93
39	1	0	2	3	103	96
40	1	0	1	0	104	99
41	1	0	0	0	105	99
42	0	0	2	2	104	97
43	0	0	3	4	103	95
44	2	1	0	4	104	94
45	0	0	2	4	104	95

Section 2

Item	Correct B	Correct G	Wrong B	Wrong G	Not attempted B	Not attempted G
1	79	74	25	25	2	0
2	94	83	9	14	3	2
3	78	80	20	16	8	3
4	84	80	20	19	2	0
5	49	63	17	21	40	15
6	38	36	66	59	2	4
7	57	60	32	24	17	15
8	69	70	32	14	5	15
9	44	52	29	25	33	22
10	51	58	53	30	2	11
11	78	68	22	21	6	10
12	40	25	48	47	18	27
13	68	53	23	23	15	23
14	62	46	20	21	24	32
15	33	37	27	29	46	33
16	55	50	27	25	24	24
17	75	63	22	29	9	7
18	25	34	31	33	50	32
19	46	52	40	31	20	16
20	57	51	32	30	17	18
21	28	14	39	33	39	52
22	30	31	36	50	40	18
23	48	51	36	28	22	20
24	27	24	30	33	49	42
25	20	24	21	19	65	56
26	29	31	20	14	57	54
27	26	27	30	36	50	36
28	31	36	45	39	30	24
29	30	25	31	25	45	49
30	11	7	36	31	59	61
31	21	13	16	21	69	65
32	22	32	28	23	56	44
33	30	40	21	11	55	48
34	22	16	12	15	72	68
35	9	3	18	27	79	69
36	10	14	17	19	79	66
37	12	6	8	14	86	79
38	14	24	11	9	81	66
39	8	9	10	10	88	80
40	8	1	9	14	89	84
41	11	6	13	18	82	75
42	4	5	13	11	89	83
43	10	6	4	4	92	89
44	6	3	6	6	94	90
45	2	1	5	6	99	92
46	5	6	5	5	96	88
47	7	6	5	6	94	87
48	6	1	8	4	92	94
49	2	1	1	2	103	96
50	2	1	4	8	100	90

TABLE 91

ANSWER PATTERNS OF ENGLISH TEST
(106 BOYS AND 99 GIRLS)

	Item	Correct		Wrong		Not attempted	
		B	G	B	G	B	G
SECTION 1	1	38	42	65	54	3	3
	2	80	83	26	15	0	1
	3	77	79	28	19	1	1
	4	78	80	28	18	0	1
	5	81	85	24	13	1	1
	6	82	86	24	12	0	1
SECTION 2	1	8	6	95	85	3	8
	2	50	59	50	34	6	6
	3	10	12	92	82	4	5
	4	43	54	57	38	6	7
	5	52	56	41	33	13	10
	6	29	35	65	56	12	8
	7	38	42	58	50	10	7
	8	58	64	42	33	6	2
	9	40	41	59	55	7	3
	10	7	7	87	83	12	9
SECTION 3	1	81	94	22	4	3	1
	2	69	81	34	17	3	1
	3	36	45	44	30	26	24
	4	47	65	54	31	5	3
	5	59	73	37	23	10	3
	6	25	33	72	62	9	4
	7	77	78	20	15	9	6
	8	48	46	43	44	15	9
	9	28	30	48	52	30	17
	10	21	33	45	40	40	26
	11	11	21	79	66	16	12
	12	21	33	69	60	16	6
	13	18	26	77	68	11	5
	14	37	49	45	35	24	15
	15	67	67	22	20	17	12
	16	57	75	37	20	12	4
	17	31	53	66	44	9	2
	18	39	55	55	40	12	4
	19	44	59	44	28	18	12
	20	53	61	47	35	6	3

TABLE 91—(CONTD)

ANSWER PATTERNS OF ENGLISH TEST
(106 BOYS AND 99 GIRLS)

	Item	Correct		Wrong		Not attempted	
		B	G	B	G	B	G
SECTION 4	1	88	91	12	7	6	1
	2	75	68	17	19	14	12
	3	61	73	29	20	16	6
	4	38	31	32	39	36	29
	5	83	91	19	7	4	1
	6	55	65	37	21	14	13
	7	60	72	39	25	7	2
	8	37	46	41	44	28	9
	9	64	67	22	23	20	9
	10	31	33	33	38	42	28
SECTION 5	1	55	45	48	50	3	4
	2	12	14	85	77	9	8
	3	67	73	30	17	9	9
	4	54	48	48	49	4	2
	5	62	65	32	27	12	7
	6	38	39	58	48	10	12
	7	62	46	37	42	7	11
	8	30	28	70	63	6	8
	9	34	41	60	39	12	19
	10	26	20	73	74	7	5

		Correct		Partly correct		Wrong		Not attempted	
		B	G	B	G	B	G	B	G
SECTION 6	1	56	66	13	7	9	11	28	15
	2	79	70	5	7	6	8	16	14
	3	22	25	19	16	23	21	42	37
	4	20	19	13	11	14	26	59	43
	5	36	35	11	5	19	21	40	38
	6	13	4	4	1	16	18	73	76
	7	22	8	23	14	12	17	49	60
	8	1	0	0	0	12	19	93	80
	9	1	1	0	0	20	12	85	86
	10	2	1	2	1	21	12	81	85

TABLE 92

RELATION BETWEEN OCCUPATION 1961 AND ARITHMETIC SCORE 1960

Numbers of young people

					Occupation				
Score	*0*	*1*	*2, 3, Y*	*4*	*5*	*6*	*7, 8, 9*	*X*	*Total*
55 and over	182	4	2	5	12	14	1	3	223
50–54	101	16	1	6	14	23	1	2	164
45–49	87	13	3	21	19	29	8		180
40–44	99	18	7	26	29	35	4		218
35–39	92	15	12	34	33	35	7		228
30–34	56	36	21	32	38	34	3	3	223
25–29	35	26	23	34	33	26	2	2	181
20–24	14	18	20	27	31	18	3	2	133
15–19	5	6	17	23	24	6			81
0–14	2	4	36	40	38	6		2	128
Unknown	13	4	4	10	6	1	1		39
Totals	686	160	146	258	277	227	30	14	1798

TABLE 93

RELATION BETWEEN OCCUPATION 1961 AND ENGLISH SCORE 1960

Numbers of young people

					Occupation				
Score	*0*	*1*	*2, 3, Y*	*4*	*5*	*6*	*7, 8, 9*	*X*	*Total*
55 and over	169	4	1	3	1	9	1		188
50–54	130	8		5	5	12	3	1	164
45–49	119	15	3	13	17	25	8		200
40–44	108	24	7	22	31	41	9	1	243
35–39	84	36	11	33	39	37	5	4	249
30–34	42	23	17	29	36	44	2	2	195
25–29	15	17	30	40	44	30	1	1	178
20–24	12	20	16	40	44	13	1	4	150
15–19	5	7	29	38	35	7			121
0–14	1	1	26	28	19	3		1	79
Unknown	1	5	6	7	6	6			31
Totals	686	160	146	258	277	227	30	14	1798

INDEX

Publications of the Scottish Council for Research in Education

56 **RISING STANDARDS IN SCOTTISH PRIMARY SCHOOLS: 1953-63** Boards £1·12½p (22/6) net
Paper 80p (16/-) net

57 **SCHOOL INSPECTION IN SCOTLAND 1840-1966**
By T R BONE, MA, MED, PHD £1·50p (30/-) net

58 **SIXTEEN YEARS ON**
By JAMES MAXWELL, MA, BED
Boards £2·10p (42/-) net
Paper £1·50p (30/-) net

59 **THE TRANSITION TO SECONDARY EDUCATION**
By J D NISBET, MA, BED, PHD and N J ENTWISTLE, BSc, PHD £1·25p (25/-) net

60 **A BIBLIOGRAPHY OF SCOTTISH EDUCATION BE-FORE 1872**
By JAMES CRAIGIE, OBE, MA, PHD, FEIS
£4·50p (90/-) net

61 **A HISTORY OF THE TRAINING OF TEACHERS IN SCOTLAND**
By MARJORIE CRUICKSHANK, MA, PHD
£2·50p (50/-) net

62 **A STUDY OF FIFTEEN-YEAR-OLDS** £2·10p (42/-) net

THE SCOTTISH PUPIL'S SPELLING BOOK
Parts I-V 10p (2/-) each   Teacher's Book 75p (15/-) each

MANUAL FOR THE SCOTTISH STANDARDISATION OF THE WECHSLER INTELLIGENCE SCALE FOR CHILD-REN 25p (5/-) net
(Available only to users of the Wechsler Scale and on application to the Council)

SCHOLASTIC SURVEY TESTS IN ENGLISH AND ARITHMETIC (as used in Publications No XLVIII, L and 56)
20 tests £1